Photomicrographs of the non-flowering plant

A. C. Shaw
Head of the Biology Department, The Skinners' School, Tunbridge Wells

S. K. Lazell, A.R.P.S.
Medical Photographer, Tunbridge Wells Hospital Group

G. N. Foster
Junior Research Associate, School of Agriculture,
University of Newcastle-upon-Tyne

LONGMANS

Longmans, Green & Co. Ltd
London and Harlow
Associated companies, branches and representatives
throughout the world

© Longmans, Green & Co. Ltd 1968

First published 1968

Made and printed in Great Britain by
William Clowes and Sons, Limited, London and Beccles

Contents

Preface

The aim of this book is basically the same as that of the companion volume, 'Photomicrographs of the Flowering Plant'; to present to students of Botany and Biology at Advanced Level a set of photomicrographs of the structure and reproduction of as wide a range of flowerless plants as they will meet in their initial studies, side by side with labelled diagrams from which they can interpret what they can see under the microscope.

We have, wherever possible, deliberately used slides of the same standard as those normally available to schools and we realise that no single photograph of a portion of material on these slides will show as much as the student can see for himself under the microscope. We have had to decide what to show in the photograph focusing at a certain depth. We hope that the drawing which accompanies each photograph presents most of the detailed structure which the student will see for himself on the slide.

The photographs were obtained with a Beck London 47 microscope and eyepiece camera using Ilford Micro-Neg. Pan. and HP3 film. The drawings were obtained by drawing over a faint print with Indian ink and bleaching out the photograph. For certain of the living preparations we have used the technique of phase-contrast microscopy. We did this to demonstrate structural detail which does not photograph satisfactorily under the light microscope.

We would not ourselves expect our students to make drawings of organisms such as *Chlamydomonas* and *Euglena* but we would expect them to make careful observations of the living organism slowed down with, for example, brilliant cresyl blue. From these observations they can obtain the information in the drawings. Future studies lead on to the examination of electron-micrographs and we have exemplified this approach with an electronmicrograph of *Chlamydomonas*.

A. C. Shaw

Tunbridge Wells, 1967

S. K. Lazell

G. N. Foster

Acknowledgements

We are grateful to the following companies for the provision of slides: T. Gerrard and Co. Ltd., Flatters and Garnett Ltd., Harris Biological Supplies Ltd. and Northern Biological Supplies. Living material was supplied from the Culture Collection of Algae and Protozoa, Cambridge. Our special thanks are due to Mr. T. A. Gerrard who at one time in the preparation of the book allowed us to borrow any slides from his complete collection, Mr. R. R. Fowell for advice on yeast morphology, Dr. W. Richards for the loan of slides, Dr. F. A. L. Clowes for his slides of beech mycorrhiza, Mr. Martin Lazell for assistance in the collection of living material, and Mr. R. A. Boulding for contributing hand-cut sections to our collection of preparations.

Fig. 35 (bottom right) is reproduced from a photograph by the late Dr. D. W. Ivimey-Cook in McLean and Cook *Textbook of Theoretical Botany*, Vol. I, Longmans. Dr. George E. Palade, of the Rockefeller Institute, New York, kindly provided us with fig. 2, the electronmicrograph of *Chlamydomonas*.

Mrs. Lazell deserves our best thanks for both her encouragement and her forbearance.

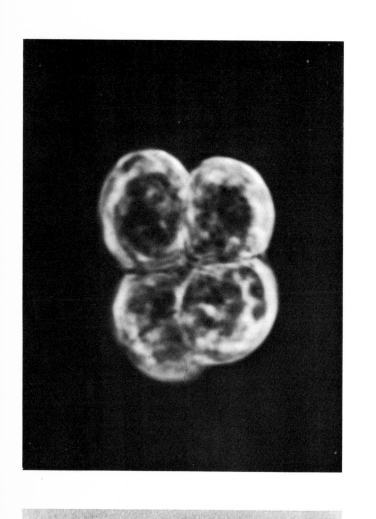

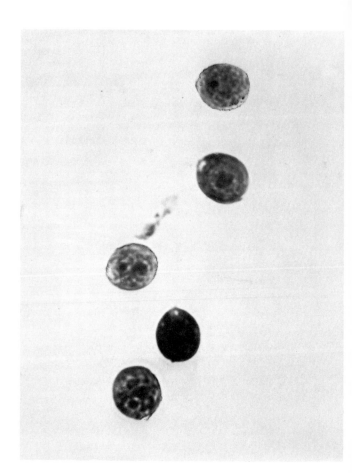

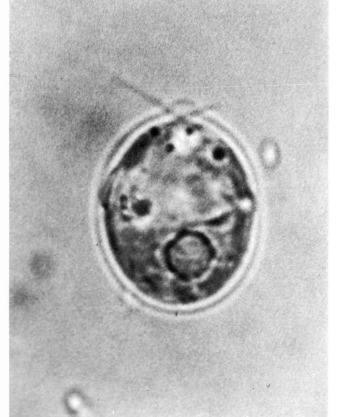

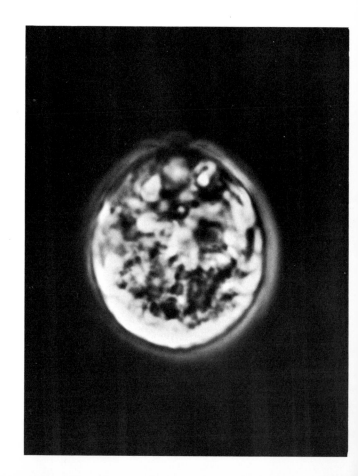

Algae

Fig. 1. High power studies of *Pleurococcus* and *Chlamydomonas*, CHLOROPHYCEAE

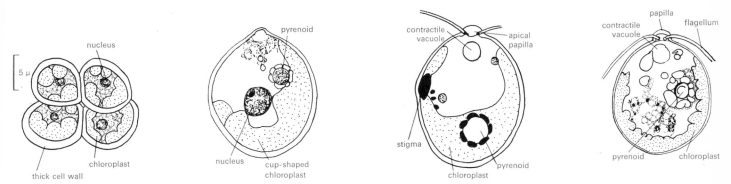

Pleurococcus—phase contrast *Chlamydomonas*—fixed preparation *Chlamydomonas*—living material, light microscope and phase contrast

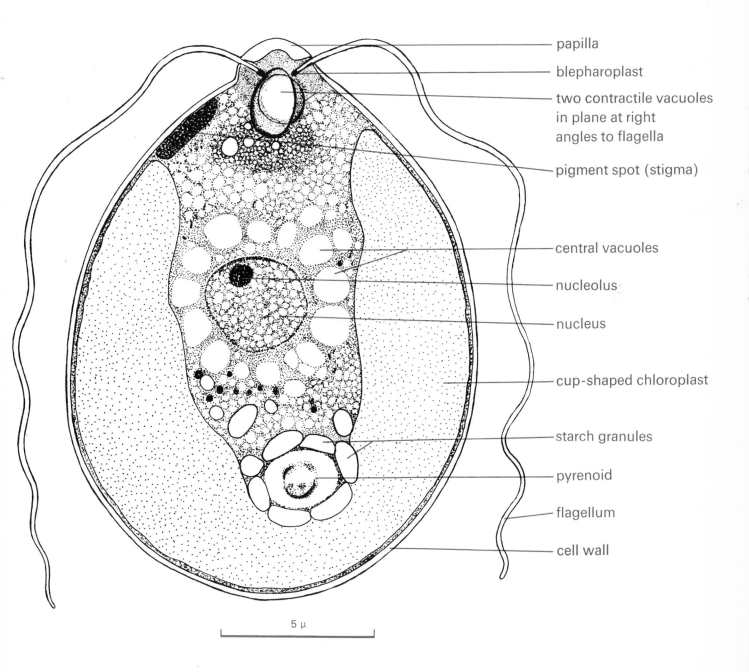

papilla

blepharoplast

two contractile vacuoles in plane at right angles to flagella

pigment spot (stigma)

central vacuoles

nucleolus

nucleus

cup-shaped chloroplast

starch granules

pyrenoid

flagellum

cell wall

5 μ

Composite drawing of *Chlamydomonas*

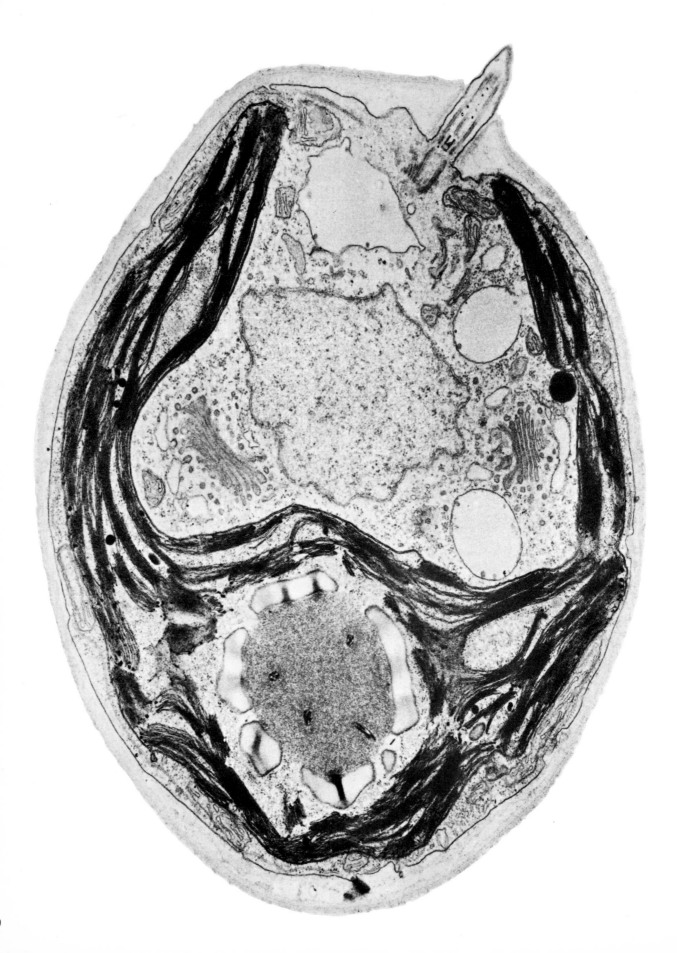

Fig. 2. Section of *Chlamydomonas reinhardi* viewed under the electron microscope (by kind permission of G. E. Palade, the Rockefeller University, New York)

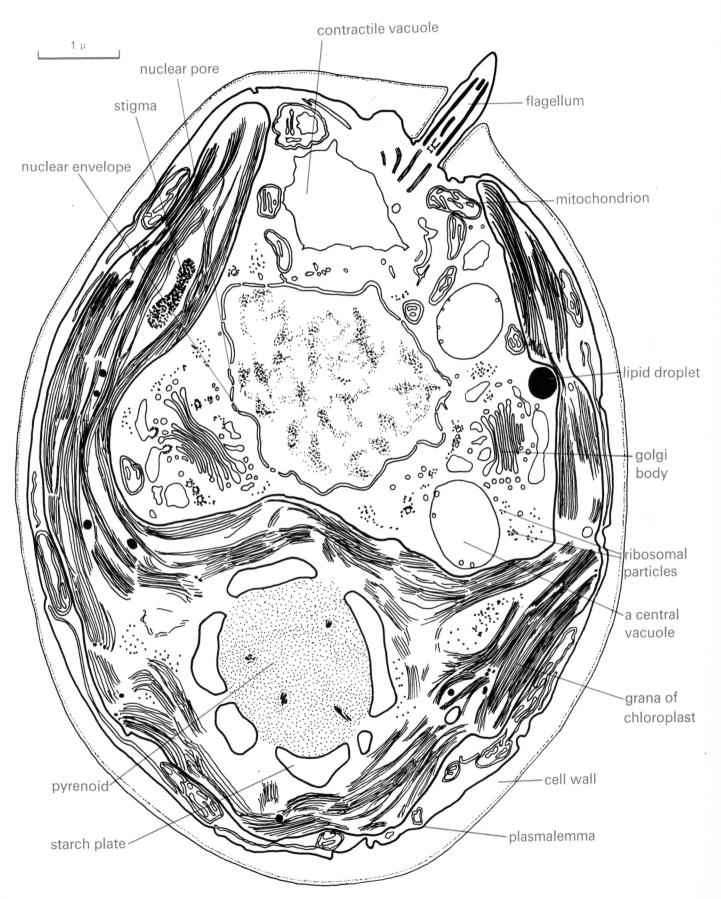

1 μ

contractile vacuole

nuclear pore

stigma

nuclear envelope

flagellum

mitochondrion

lipid droplet

golgi body

ribosomal particles

a central vacuole

grana of chloroplast

cell wall

plasmalemma

pyrenoid

starch plate

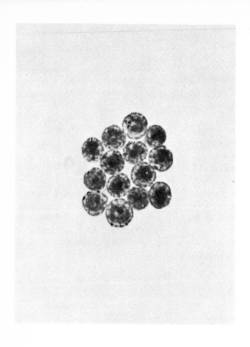
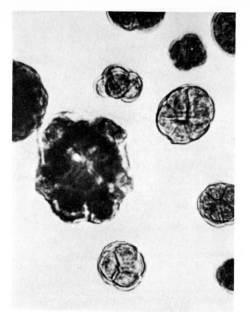
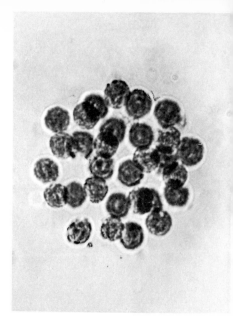
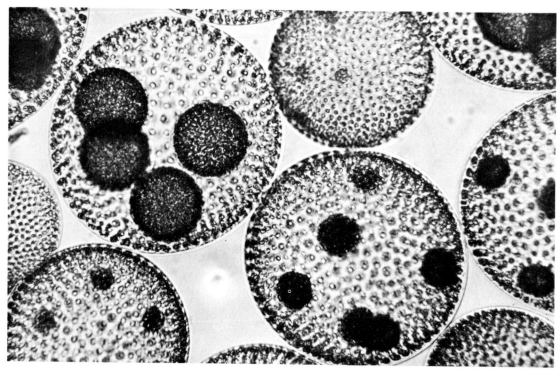
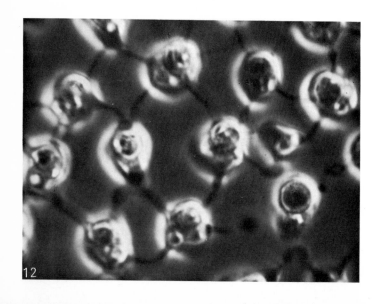
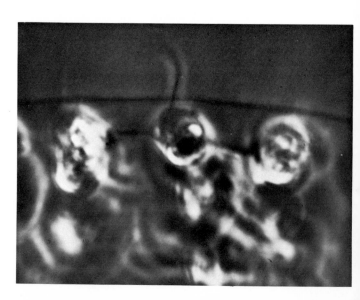

12

Fig. 3.   High power studies of vegetative structure in Volvocales, CHLOROPHYCEAE

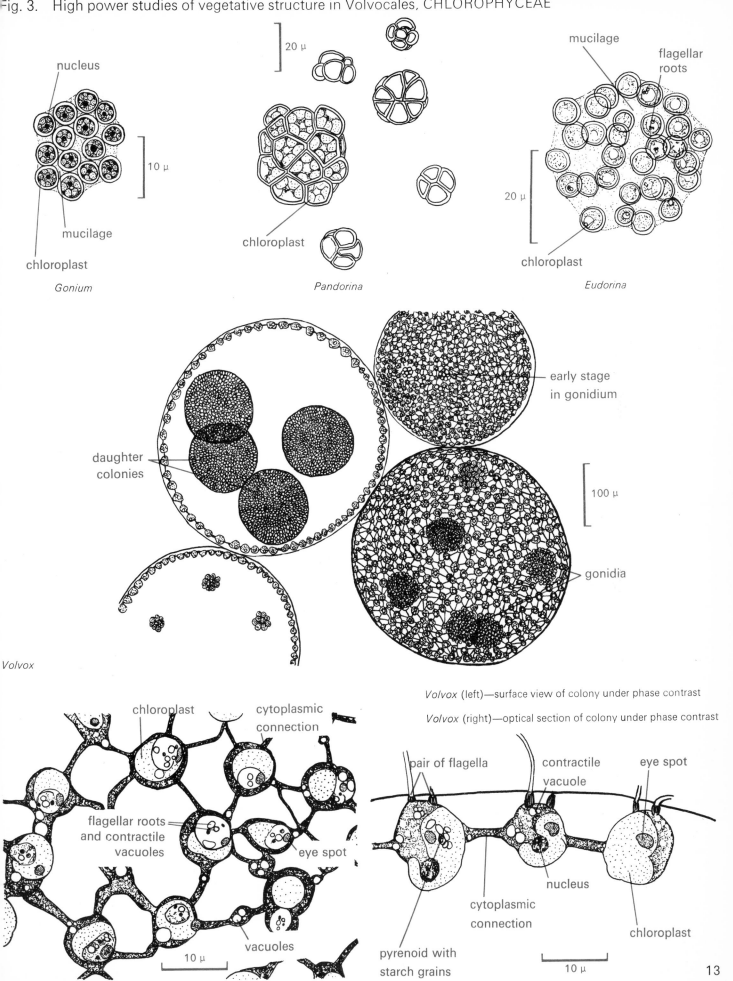

20 μ

nucleus

10 μ

mucilage

chloroplast

Gonium

chloroplast

Pandorina

mucilage

flagellar roots

20 μ

chloroplast

Eudorina

daughter colonies

early stage in gonidium

100 μ

gonidia

Volvox

Volvox (left)—surface view of colony under phase contrast

Volvox (right)—optical section of colony under phase contrast

chloroplast

cytoplasmic connection

flagellar roots and contractile vacuoles

eye spot

vacuoles

10 μ

pair of flagella

contractile vacuole

eye spot

cytoplasmic connection

nucleus

pyrenoid with starch grains

chloroplast

10 μ

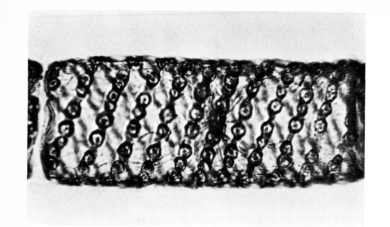
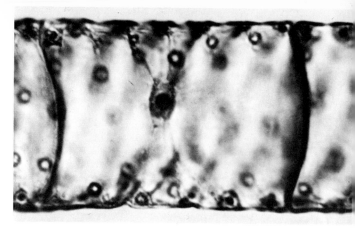
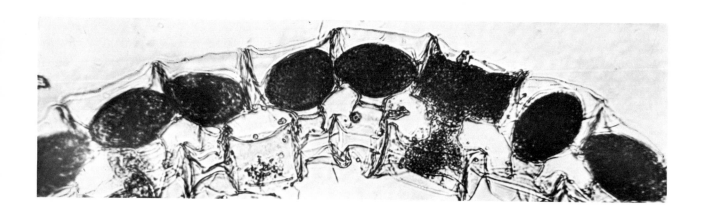
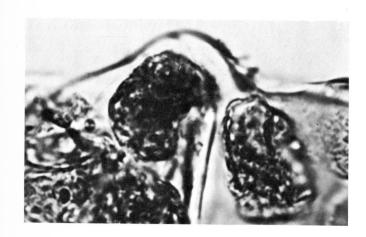
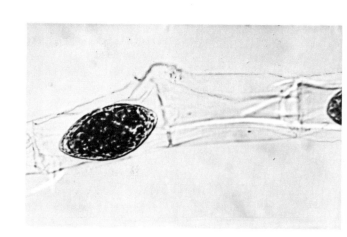
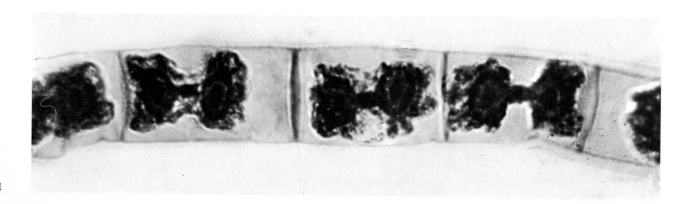

Fig. 4.   High power studies of structure and reproduction in Conjugales, CHLOROPHYCEAE

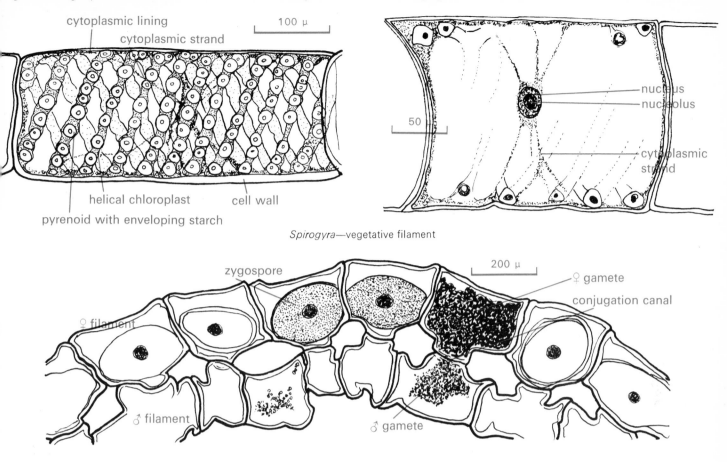

cytoplasmic lining
cytoplasmic strand
100 μ

helical chloroplast   cell wall

pyrenoid with enveloping starch

nucleus
nucleolus
50

cytoplasmic strand

Spirogyra—vegetative filament

zygospore   200 μ   ♀ gamete

conjugation canal

♀ filament

♂ filament   ♂ gamete

Spirogyra—scalariform conjugation

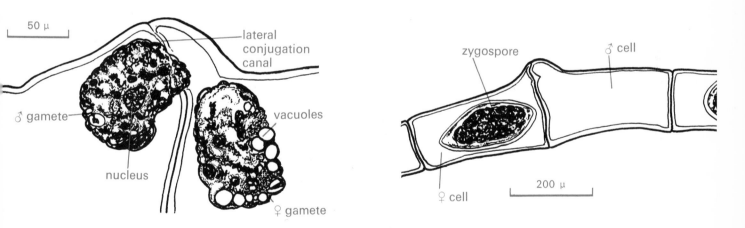

50 μ

lateral conjugation canal

♂ gamete

vacuoles

nucleus

♀ gamete

zygospore   ♂ cell

♀ cell   200 μ

Spirogyra—lateral conjugation

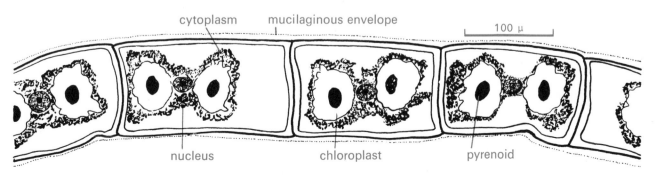

cytoplasm   mucilaginous envelope

100 μ

nucleus   chloroplast   pyrenoid

Zygnema—vegetative filament

15

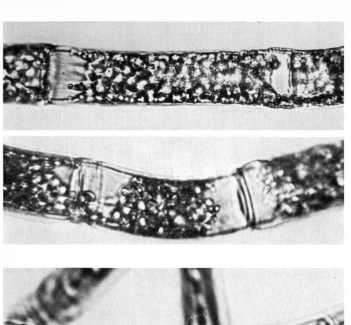

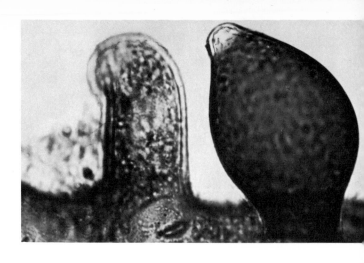

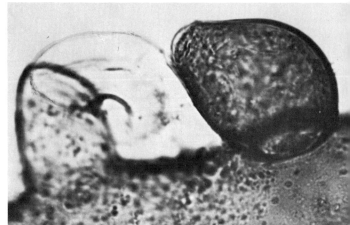

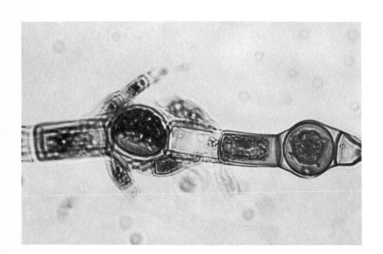

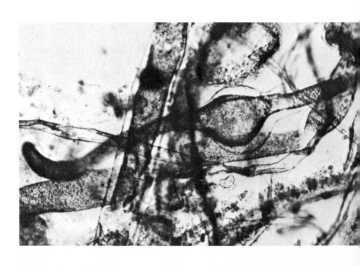

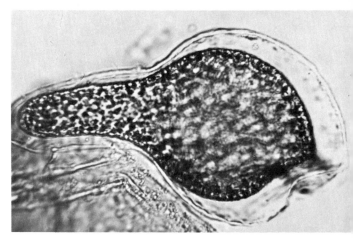

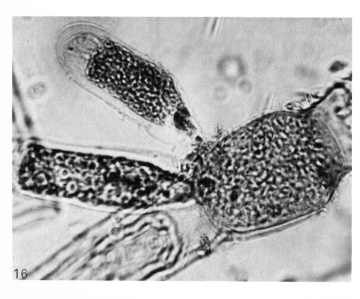

16

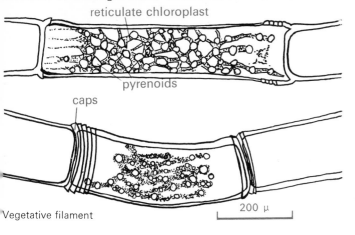

reticulate chloroplast

pyrenoids

caps

Vegetative filament

200 μ

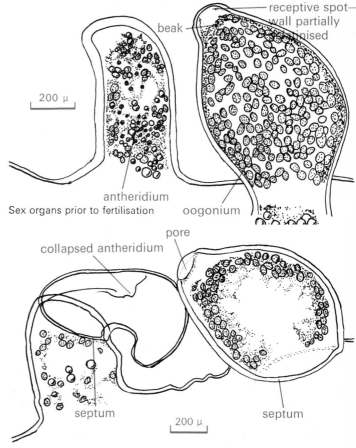

beak

receptive spot
wall partially
organised

antheridium

oogonium

200 μ

Sex organs prior to fertilisation

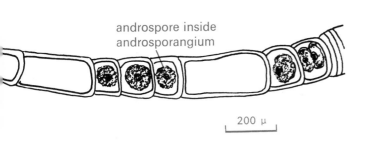

androspore inside
androsporangium

200 μ

Androsporangia

collapsed antheridium

pore

septum

septum

200 μ

Sex organs after fertilisation

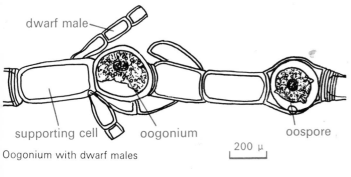

dwarf male

supporting cell

oogonium

oospore

200 μ

Oogonium with dwarf males

zoospore wall

tubular outgrowth

0·5 mm

Germinating zoospore

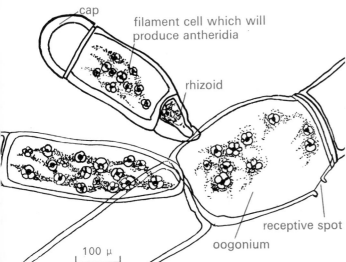

cap

filament cell which will
produce antheridia

rhizoid

receptive spot

oogonium

100 μ

Details of dwarf male attached to oogonium

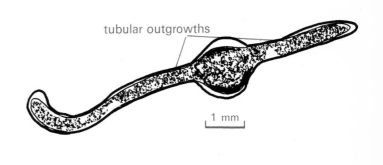

tubular outgrowths

1 mm

Germinating zoospore—later stage

17

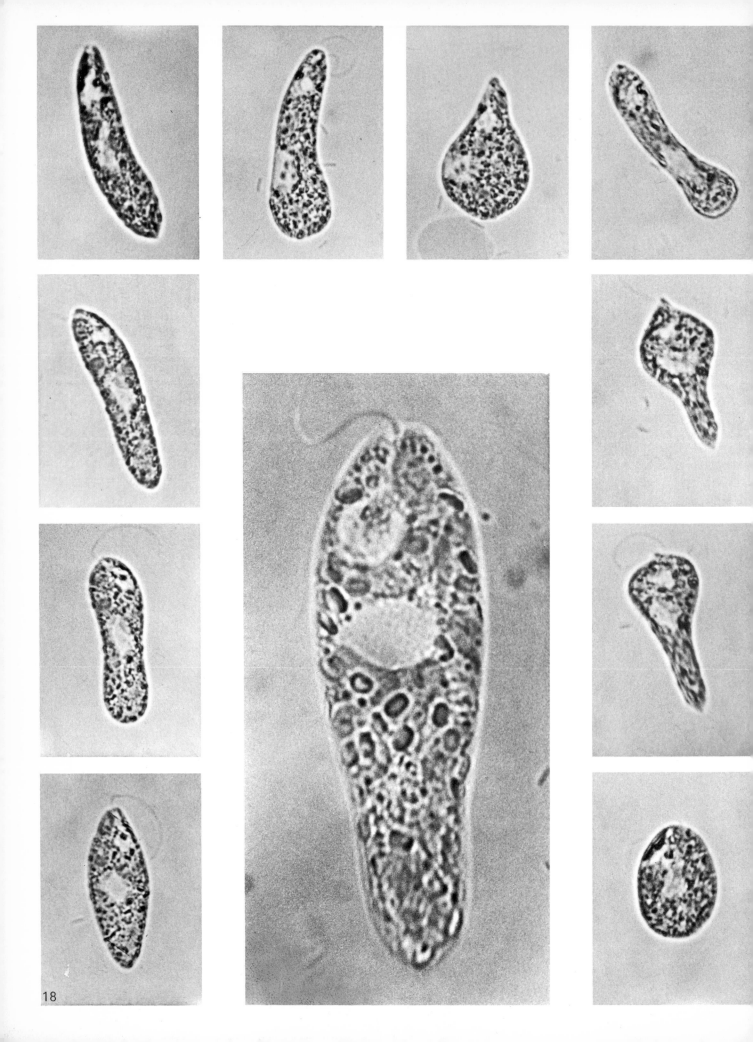

18

Fig. 7.   Light microscope studies of living *Euglena gracilis*, EUGLENOPHYCEAE

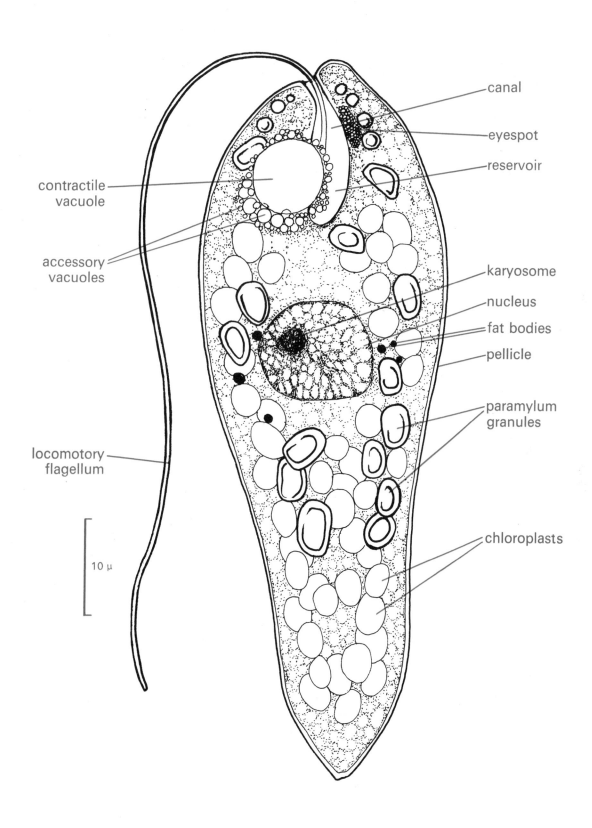

canal

eyespot

reservoir

contractile
vacuole

accessory
vacuoles

karyosome

nucleus

fat bodies

pellicle

paramylum
granules

locomotory
flagellum

10 μ

chloroplasts

A drawing of *Euglena gracilis* showing only those structures normally
visible with the aid of the light microscope
The small photographs arranged clockwise demonstrate euglenoid movement

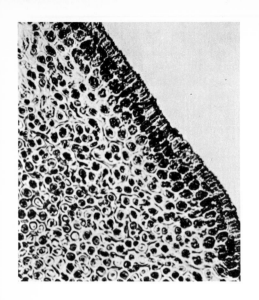
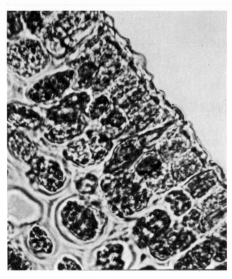
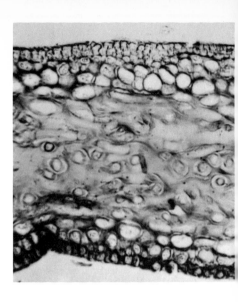
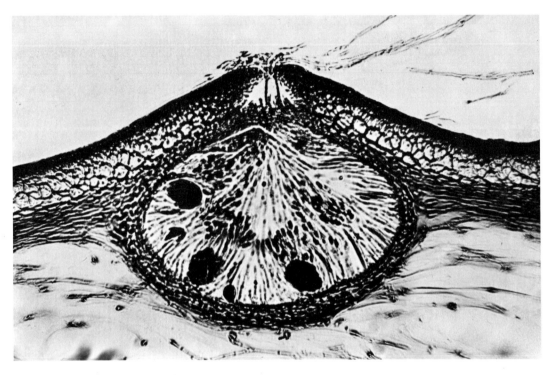
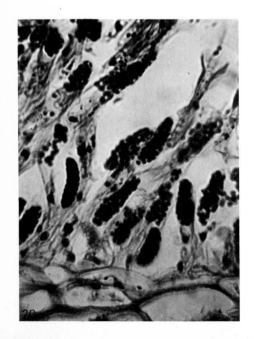
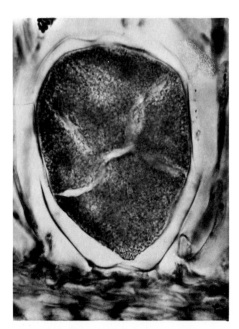

Fig. 8.   Studies of the structure and reproduction of *Fucus*, PHAEOPHYCEAE

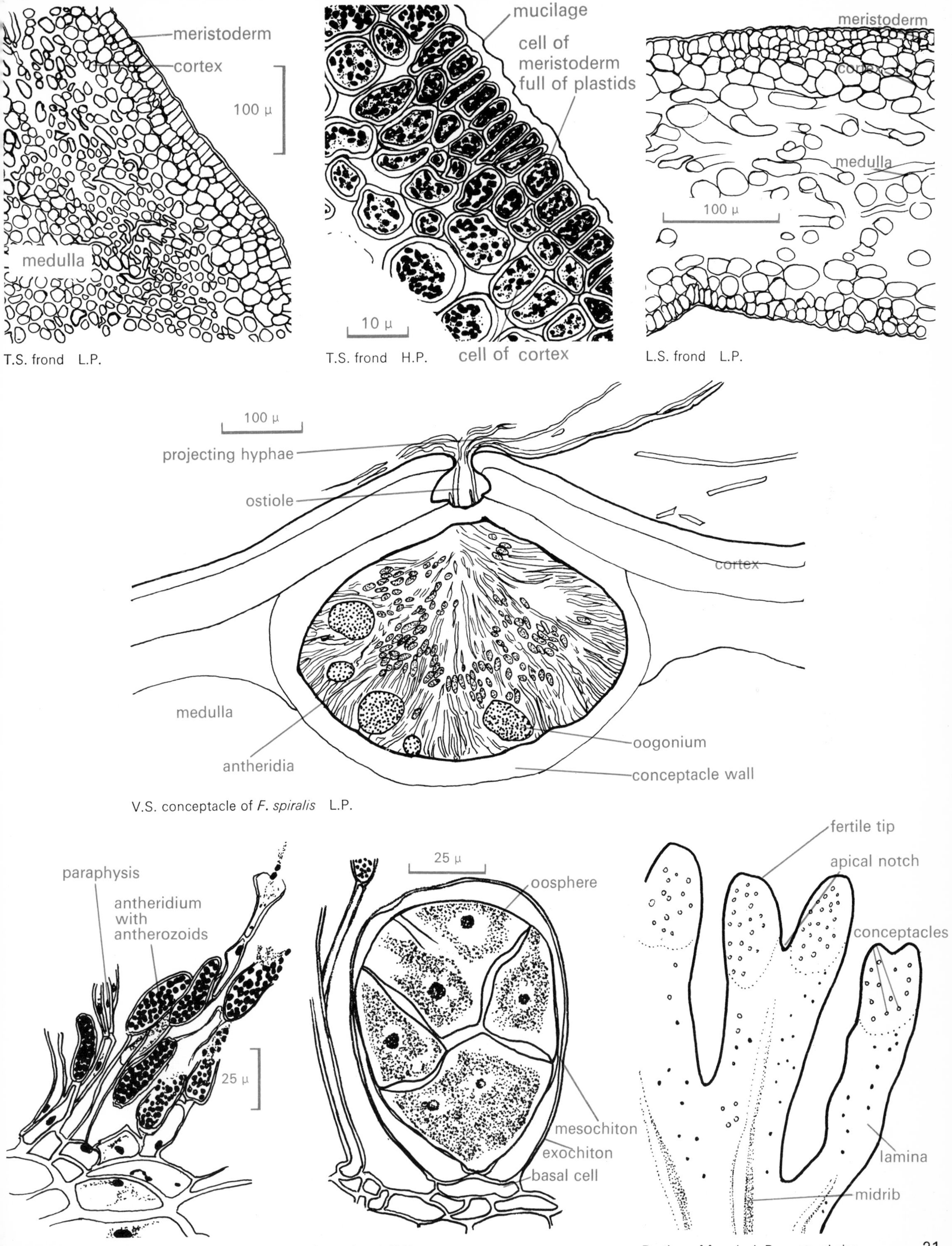

meristoderm
cortex
100 μ
medulla

T.S. frond   L.P.

mucilage
cell of meristoderm full of plastids
10 μ
cell of cortex

T.S. frond   H.P.

meristoderm
cortex
medulla
100 μ

L.S. frond   L.P.

100 μ
projecting hyphae
ostiole
cortex
medulla
antheridia
oogonium
conceptacle wall

V.S. conceptacle of *F. spiralis*   L.P.

paraphysis
antheridium with antherozoids
25 μ

Antheridia   H.P.

25 μ
oosphere
mesochiton
exochiton
basal cell

Oogonium   H.P.

fertile tip
apical notch
conceptacles
lamina
midrib

Portion of frond   L.P.—natural size

21

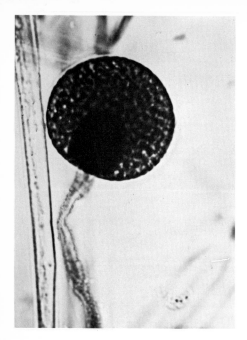

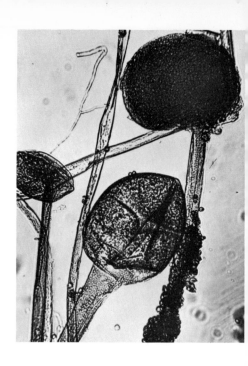

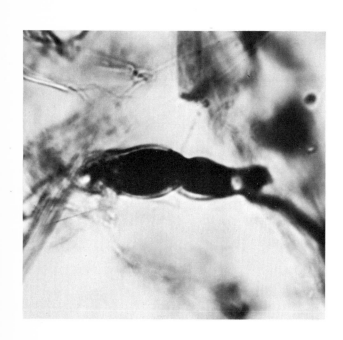
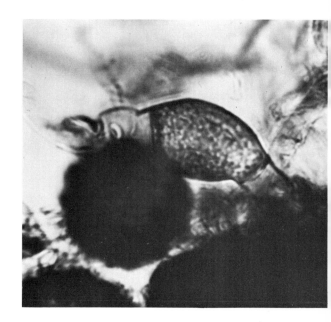

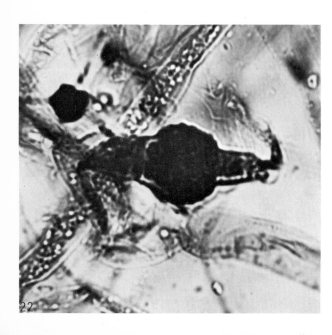

Fig. 9.   High power studies of asexual and sexual reproductive stages in *Mucor* and *Rhizopus*, PHYCOMYCETES

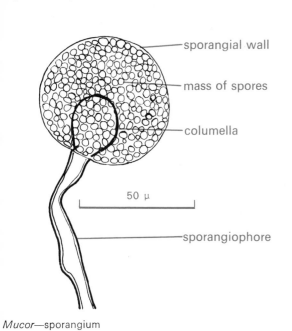

sporangial wall

mass of spores

columella

50 μ

sporangiophore

Mucor—sporangium

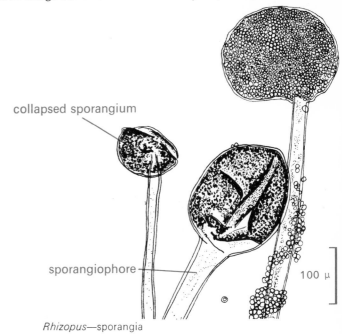

collapsed sporangium

sporangiophore

100 μ

Rhizopus—sporangia

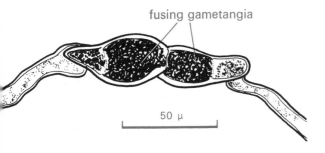

fusing gametangia

50 μ

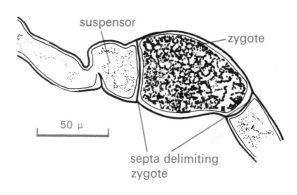

suspensor

zygote

50 μ

septa delimiting zygote

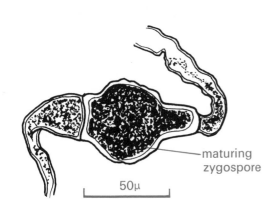

maturing zygospore

50μ

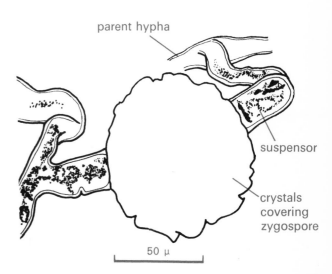

parent hypha

suspensor

crystals covering zygospore

50 μ

Mucor—stages in conjugation

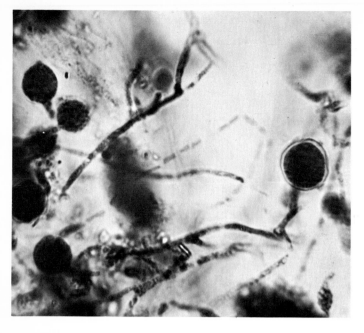
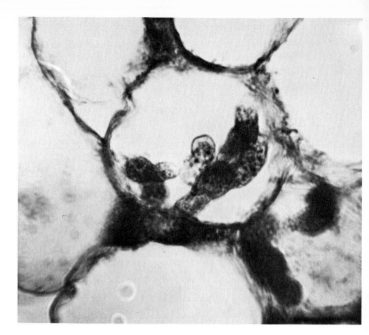

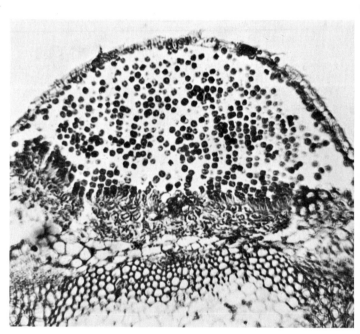
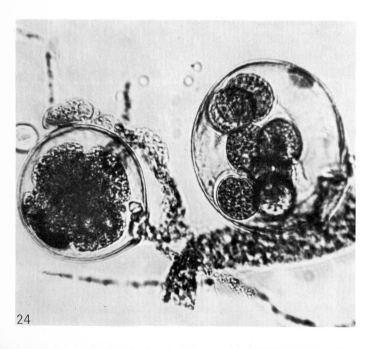
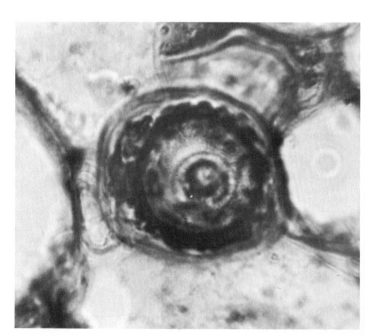

24

Fig. 10. High power studies of structure and reproduction in *Pythium, Peronospora, Cystopus,* and *Saprolegnia,* PHYCOMYCETES

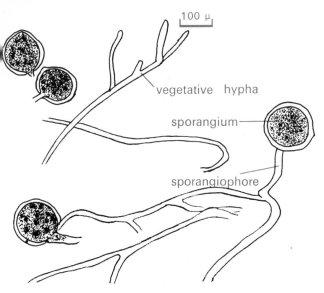

100 μ

vegetative hypha

sporangium

sporangiophore

Pythium—sporangium

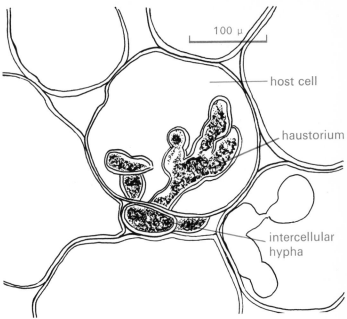

100 μ

host cell

haustorium

intercellular hypha

Peronospora—mycelium showing haustoria

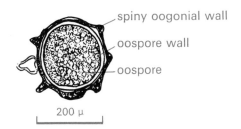

spiny oogonial wall

oospore wall

oospore

200 μ

Pythium—oospore

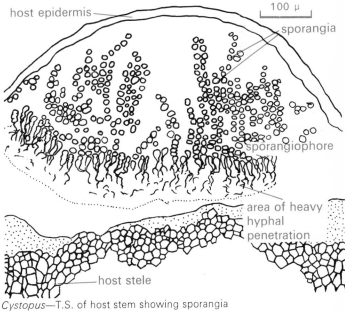

host epidermis

100 μ

sporangia

sporangiophore

area of heavy hyphal penetration

host stele

Cystopus—T.S. of host stem showing sporangia

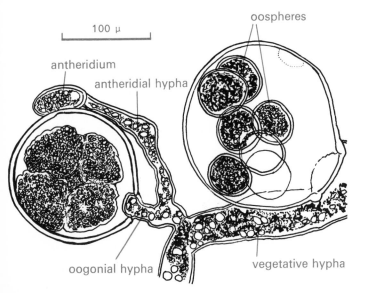

100 μ

oospheres

antheridium

antheridial hypha

oogonial hypha

vegetative hypha

Saprolegnia—antheridium, oogonium and oospheres

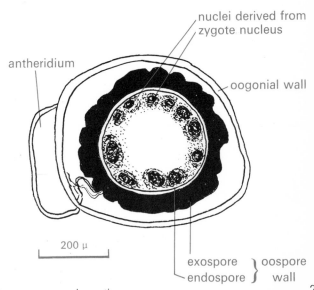

nuclei derived from zygote nucleus

antheridium

oogonial wall

200 μ

exospore } oospore
endospore } wall

Cystopus—oospore in section

25

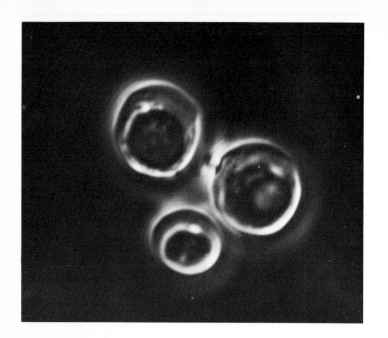

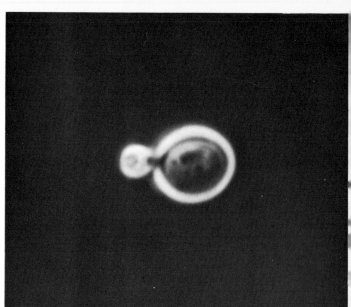

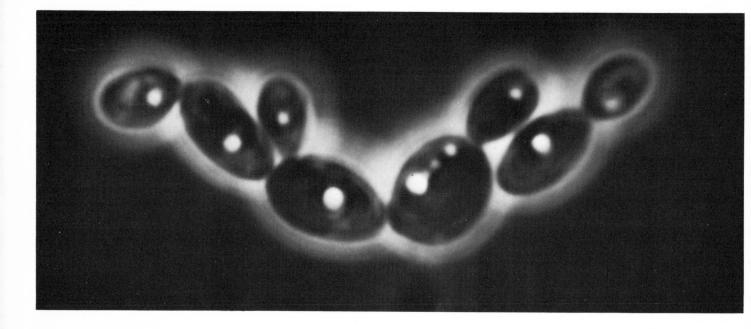

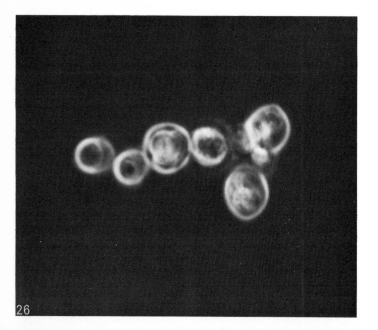

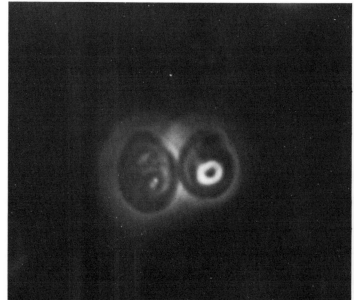

Fig. 11.   Phase contrast studies of *Saccharomyces*, ASCOMYCETES

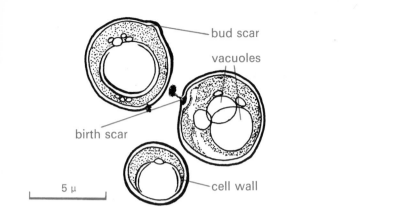

bud scar

vacuoles

birth scar

cell wall

5 μ

Vegetative cells

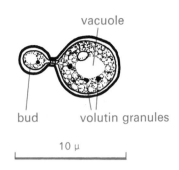

vacuole

bud

volutin granules

10 μ

Budding

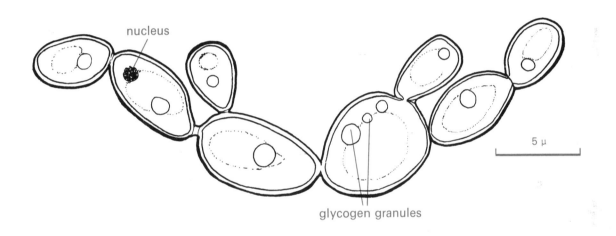

nucleus

glycogen granules

5 μ

Pseudomycelium

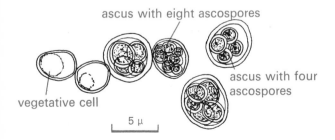

ascus with eight ascospores

ascus with four ascospores

vegetative cell

5 μ

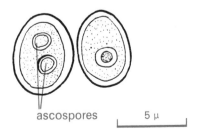

ascospores

5 μ

Asci

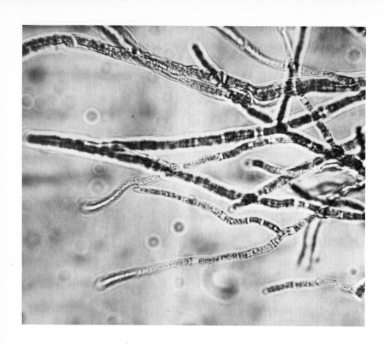

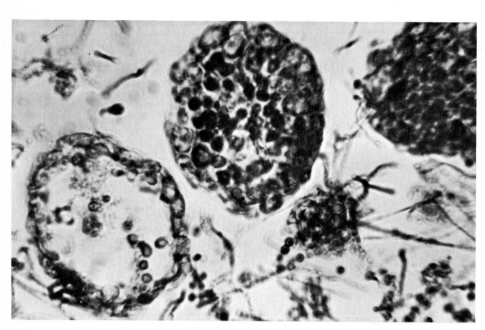

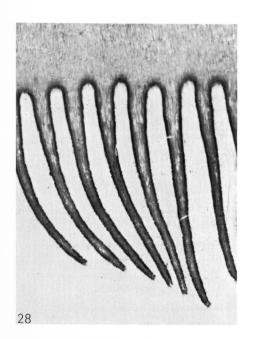
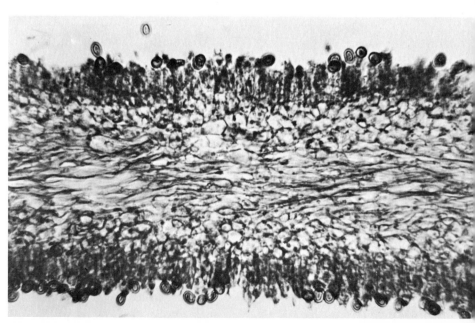

Fig. 12. High Power studies of *Aspergillus* (*Eurotium*), ASCOMYCETES

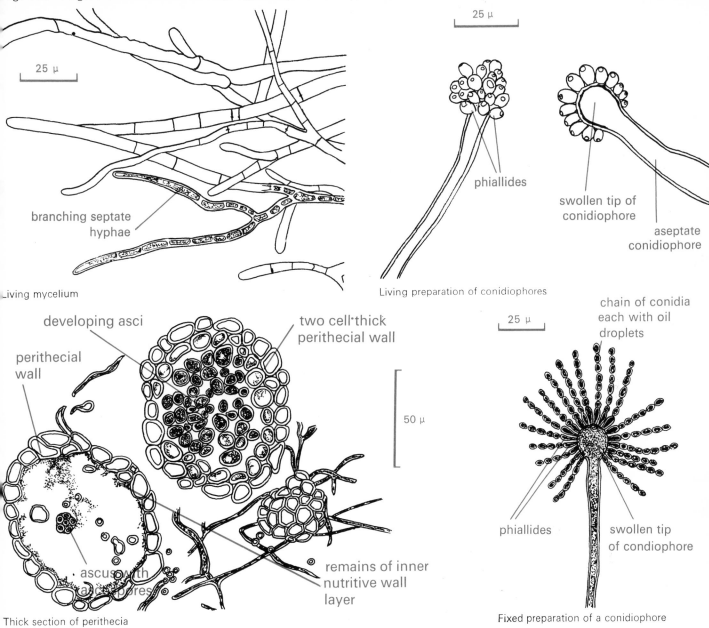

25 μ

25 μ

phiallides

swollen tip of
conidiophore

aseptate
conidiophore

branching septate
hyphae

Living mycelium

Living preparation of conidiophores

developing asci

two cell thick
perithecial wall

peritnecial
wall

50 μ

chain of conidia
each with oil
droplets

25 μ

phiallides

swollen tip
of condiophore

ascus with
ascospores

remains of inner
nutritive wall
layer

Thick section of perithecia

Fixed preparation of a conidiophore

Fig. 13. Studies of a section through the pileus of *Psalliota hortensis*, BASIDIOMYCETES

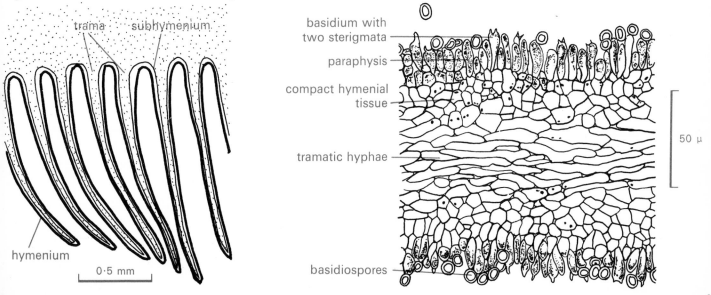

trama   subhymenium

basidium with
two sterigmata

paraphysis

compact hymenial
tissue

tramatic hyphae

50 μ

hymenium

basidiospores

0·5 mm

Vertical section   L.P.

V.S. portion of a gill   H.P.

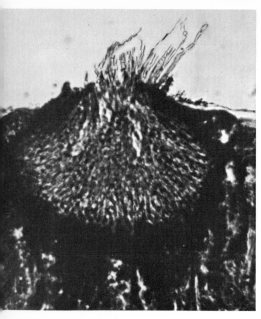
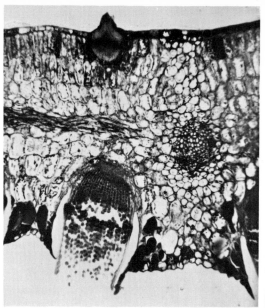
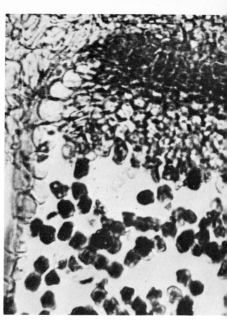
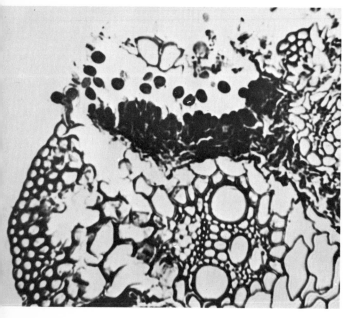
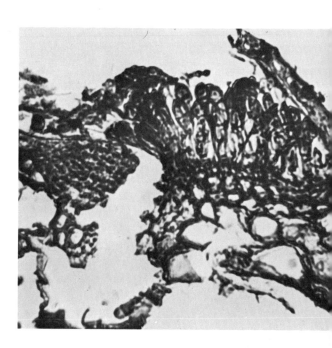
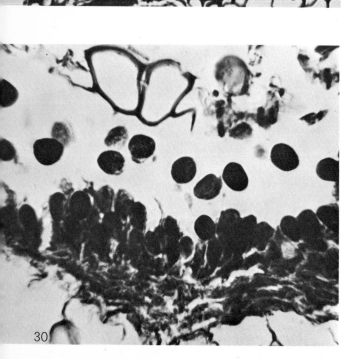

Fig. 14. Sporulating stages of *Puccinia graminis*, BASIDIOMYCETES

50 μ

long flexuous
receptive
hyphae

pycnospores

-forming
ue

host tissue

V.S. pycnidium   H.P.

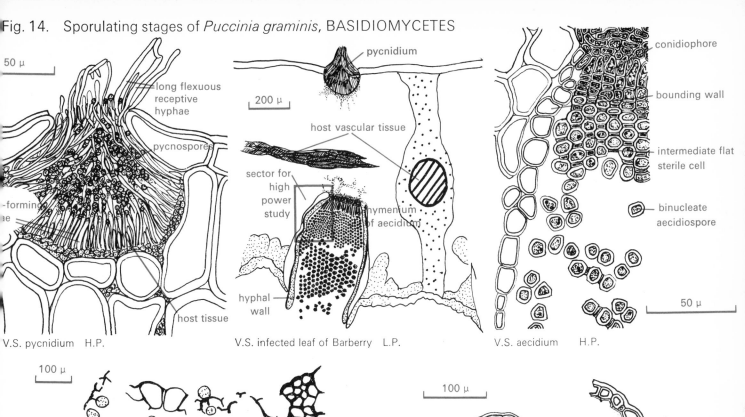

pycnidium

200 μ

host vascular tissue

sector for
high
power
study

hymenium
of aecidium

hyphal
wall

V.S. infected leaf of Barberry   L.P.

conidiophore

bounding wall

intermediate flat
sterile cell

binucleate
aecidiospore

50 μ

V.S. aecidium   H.P.

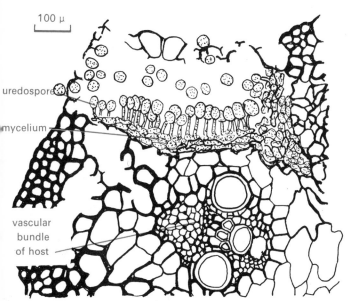

100 μ

uredospore

mycelium

vascular
bundle
of host

V.S. uredosorus on wheat   L.P.

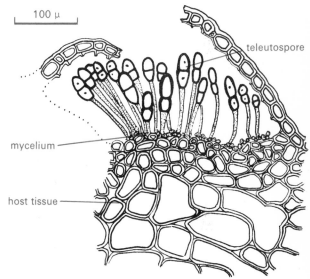

100 μ

teleutospore

mycelium

host tissue

V.S. teleutosorus on wheat   L.P.

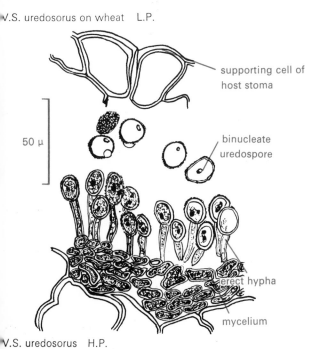

supporting cell of
host stoma

binucleate
uredospore

50 μ

erect hypha

mycelium

V.S. uredosorus   H.P.

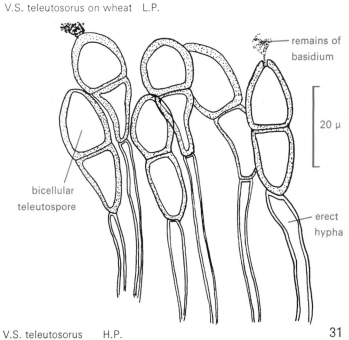

remains of
basidium

20 μ

bicellular
teleutospore

erect
hypha

V.S. teleutosorus   H.P.

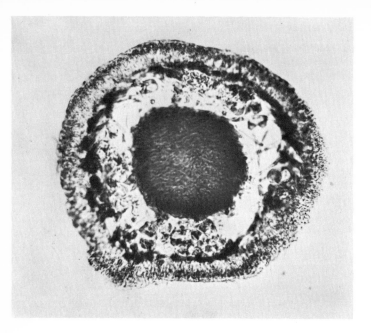

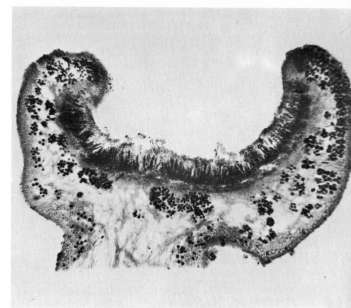

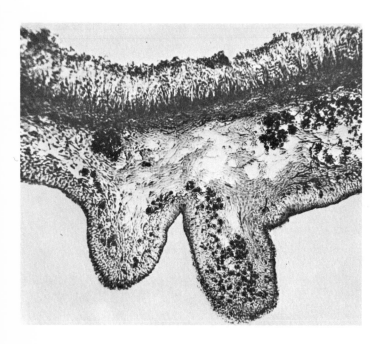

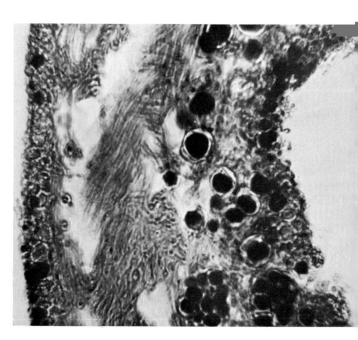

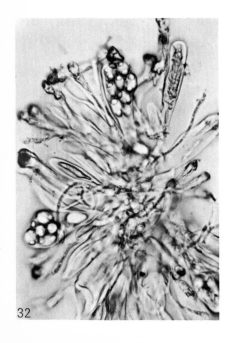

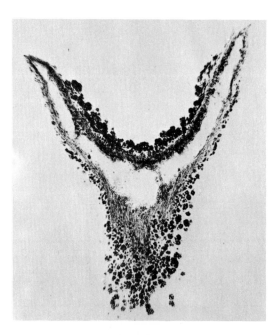

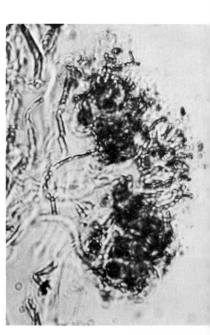

32

Lichenes

Fig. 15. Studies of ascomycete lichens

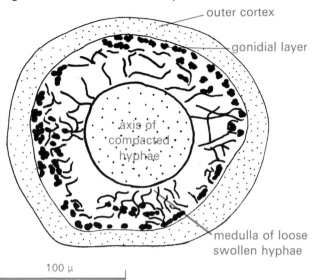

T.S. thallus of a fruticose lichen, *Usnea* L.P.

outer cortex

gonidial layer

axis of compacted hyphae

medulla of loose swollen hyphae

100 μ

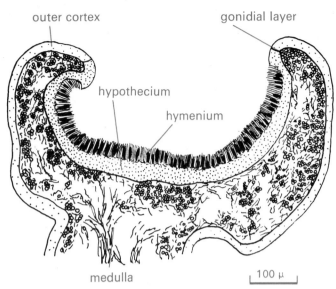

V.S. apothecium of a foliose lichen, *Parmelia* (*Hypogymnia*) L.P.

outer cortex

gonidial layer

hypothecium

hymenium

medulla

100 μ

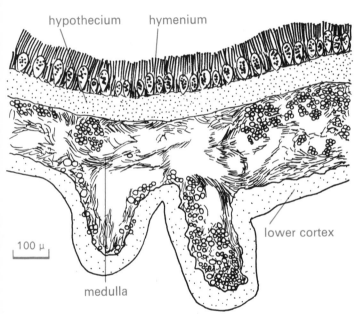

V.S. apothecium of a foliose lichen, *Xanthoria* L.P.

hypothecium

hymenium

lower cortex

medulla

100 μ

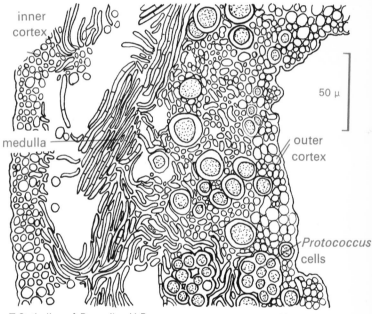

T.S. thallus of *Parmelia* H.P.

inner cortex

medulla

outer cortex

Protococcus cells

50 μ

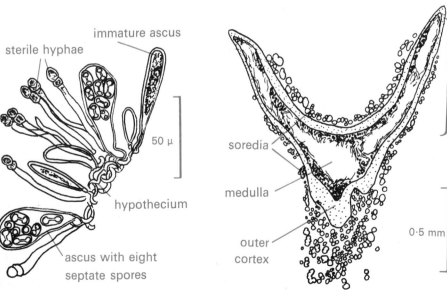

Macerated hymenium of *Xanthoria* H.P.

sterile hyphae

immature ascus

50 μ

hypothecium

ascus with eight septate spores

V.S. podetium of *Cladonia* L.P.

scyphus

soredia

medulla

outer cortex

0·5 mm

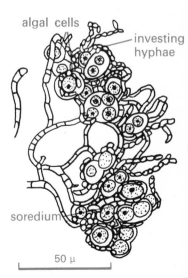

Soredia of *Cladonia* H.P.

algal cells

investing hyphae

soredium

50 μ

3

33

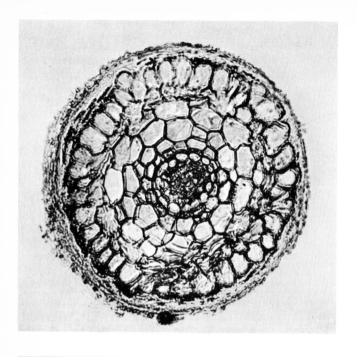

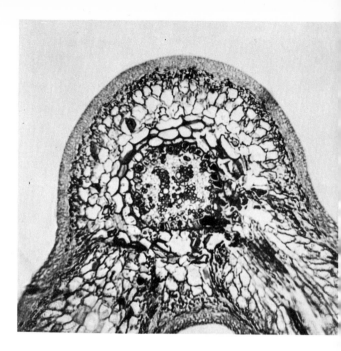

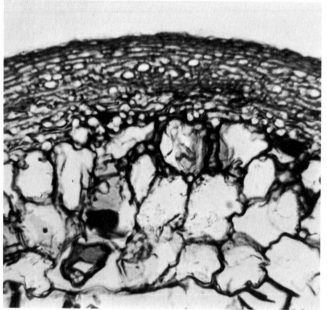

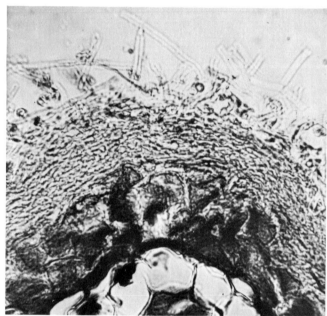

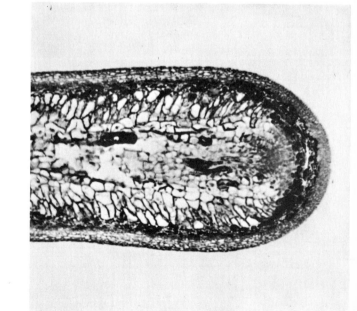

Mycorrhiza

Fig. 16. Studies of the ectotrophic mycorrhiza of the root of *Fagus sylvatica*, the Beech

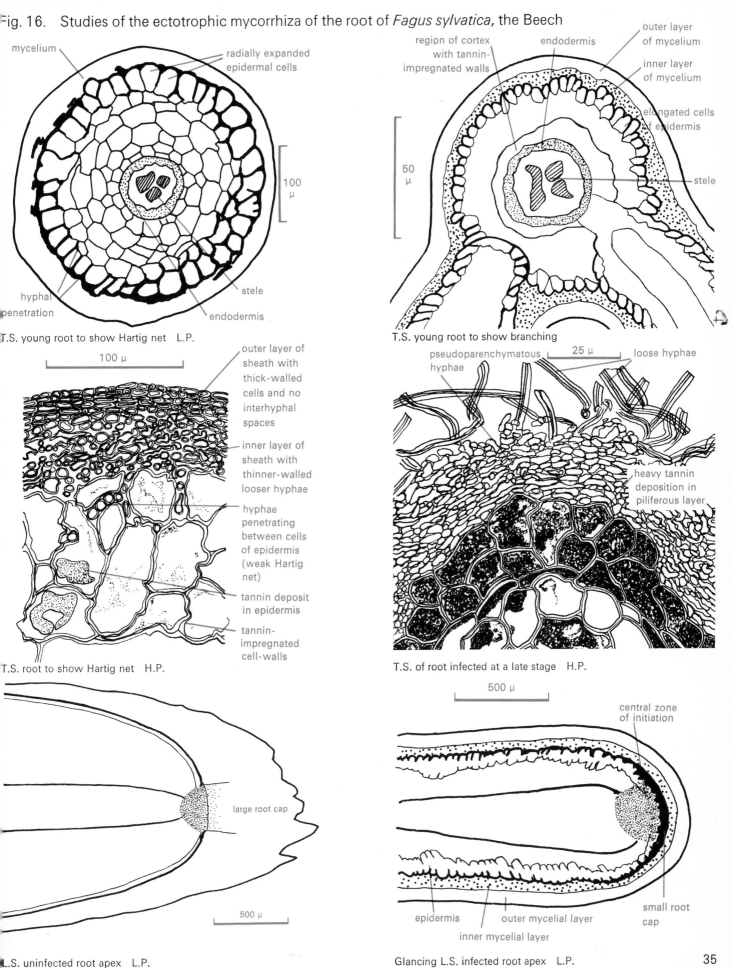

mycelium

radially expanded
epidermal cells

100
µ

hyphal
penetration

stele

endodermis

T.S. young root to show Hartig net   L.P.

region of cortex
with tannin-
impregnated walls

endodermis

outer layer
of mycelium

inner layer
of mycelium

elongated cells
of epidermis

stele

50
µ

T.S. young root to show branching

100 µ

outer layer of
sheath with
thick-walled
cells and no
interhyphal
spaces

inner layer of
sheath with
thinner-walled
looser hyphae

hyphae
penetrating
between cells
of epidermis
(weak Hartig
net)

tannin deposit
in epidermis

tannin-
impregnated
cell-walls

T.S. root to show Hartig net   H.P.

pseudoparenchymatous
hyphae

25 µ

loose hyphae

heavy tannin
deposition in
piliferous layer

T.S. of root infected at a late stage   H.P.

500 µ

large root cap

central zone
of initiation

small root
cap

500 µ

epidermis

outer mycelial layer

inner mycelial layer

L.S. uninfected root apex   L.P.

Glancing L.S. infected root apex   L.P.

35

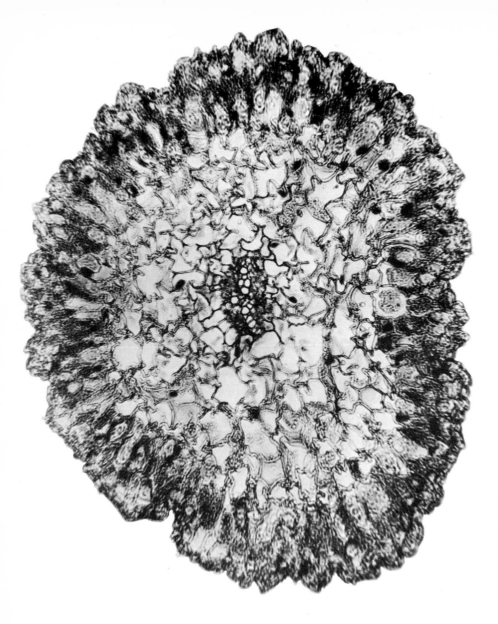

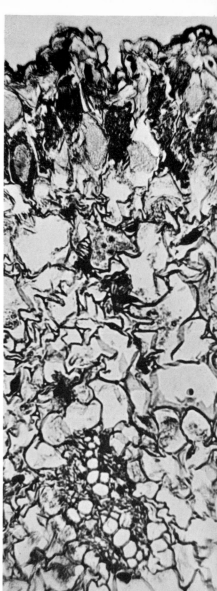

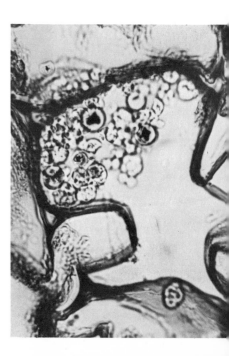

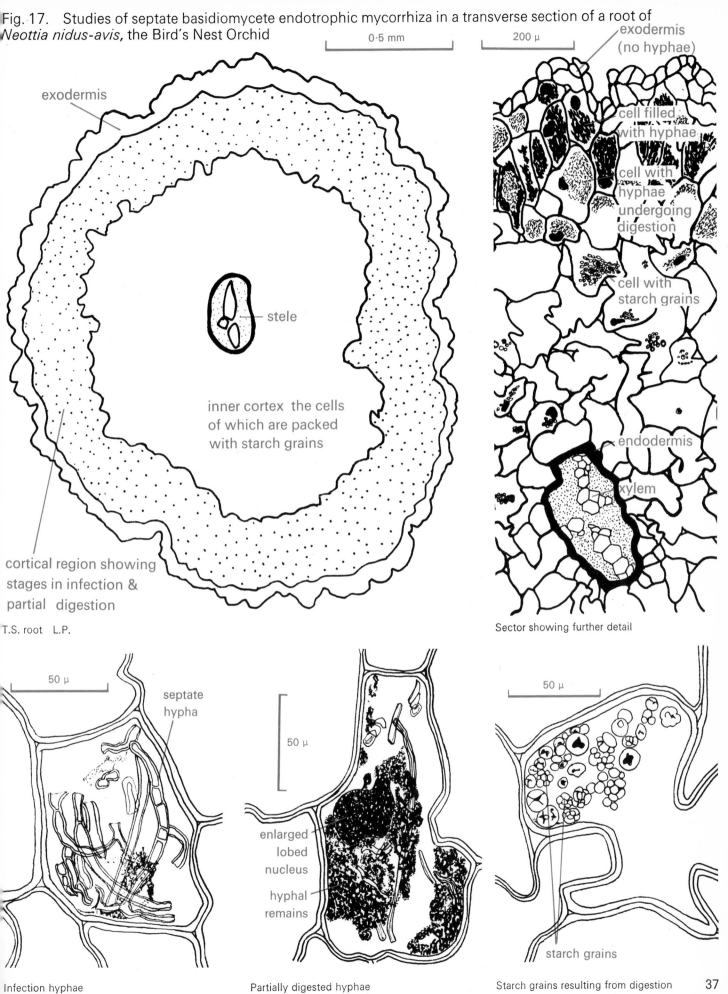

Fig. 17. Studies of septate basidiomycete endotrophic mycorrhiza in a transverse section of a root of *Neottia nidus-avis*, the Bird's Nest Orchid

0·5 mm   200 μ

exodermis (no hyphae)

exodermis

cell filled with hyphae

cell with hyphae undergoing digestion

cell with starch grains

stele

inner cortex the cells of which are packed with starch grains

endodermis

xylem

cortical region showing stages in infection & partial digestion

T.S. root L.P.

Sector showing further detail

50 μ

septate hypha

50 μ

enlarged lobed nucleus

hyphal remains

50 μ

starch grains

Infection hyphae   Partially digested hyphae   Starch grains resulting from digestion   37

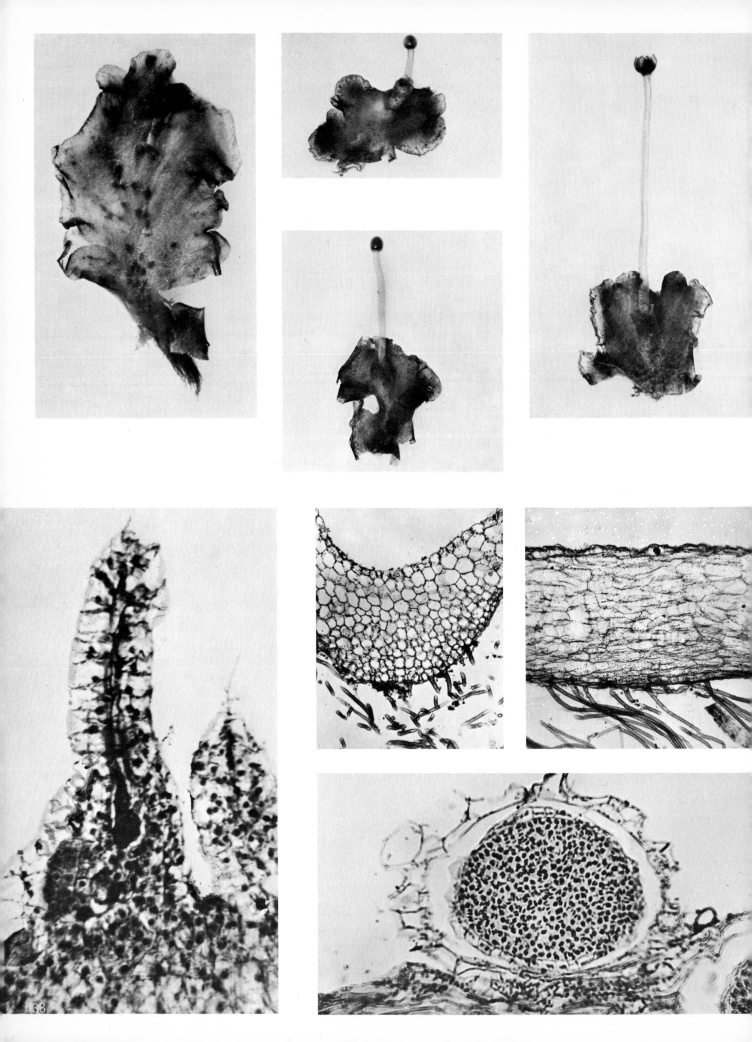

Bryophyta-Hepaticae

Fig. 18. Life studies of *Pellia epiphylla*, METZGERIALES

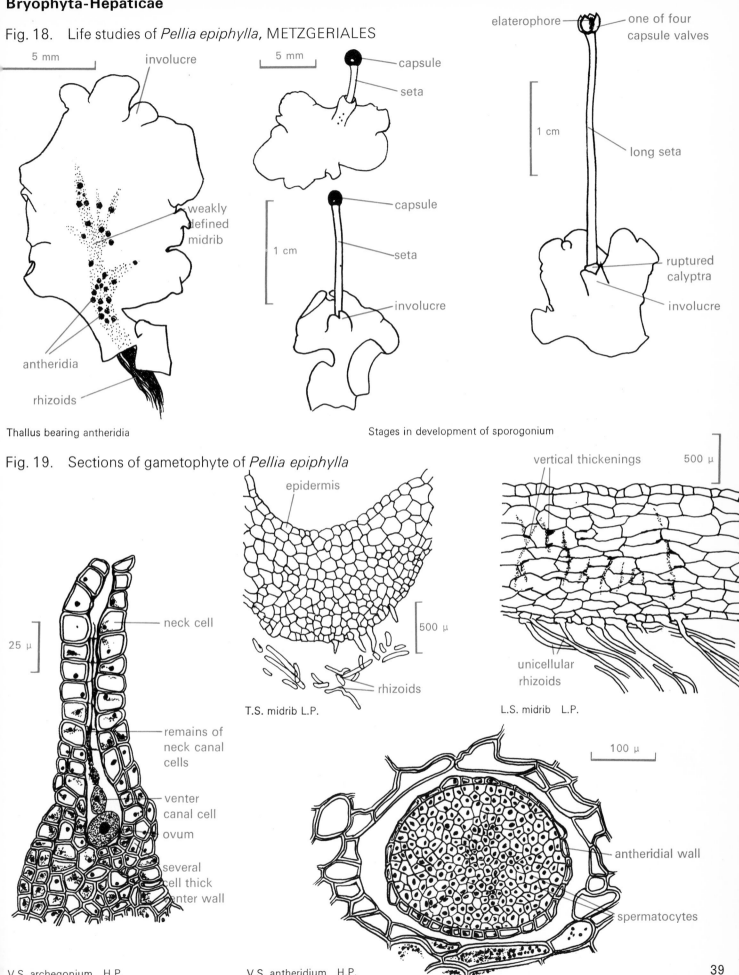

5 mm

involucre

5 mm

capsule

seta

1 cm

capsule

seta

involucre

elaterophore

one of four capsule valves

1 cm

long seta

ruptured calyptra

involucre

weakly defined midrib

antheridia

rhizoids

Thallus bearing antheridia

Stages in development of sporogonium

Fig. 19. Sections of gametophyte of *Pellia epiphylla*

epidermis

vertical thickenings

500 μ

neck cell

25 μ

remains of neck canal cells

venter canal cell

ovum

several cell thick venter wall

500 μ

rhizoids

T.S. midrib L.P.

unicellular rhizoids

L.S. midrib L.P.

100 μ

antheridial wall

spermatocytes

V.S. archegonium H.P.

V.S. antheridium H.P.

39

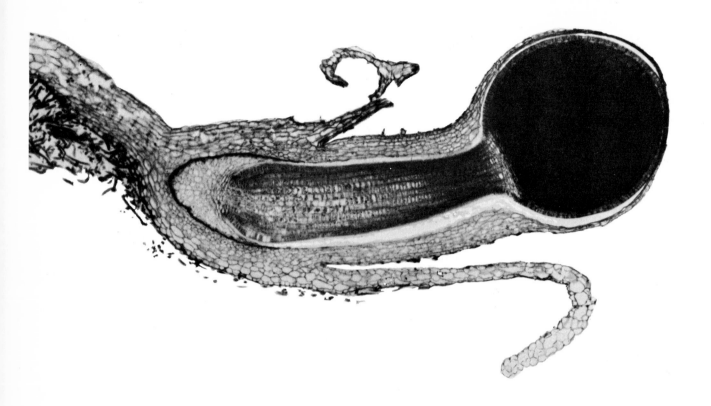

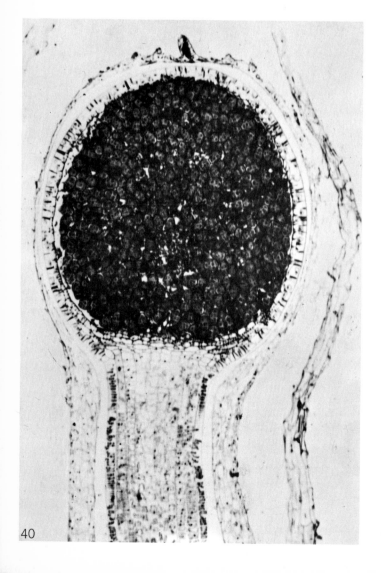

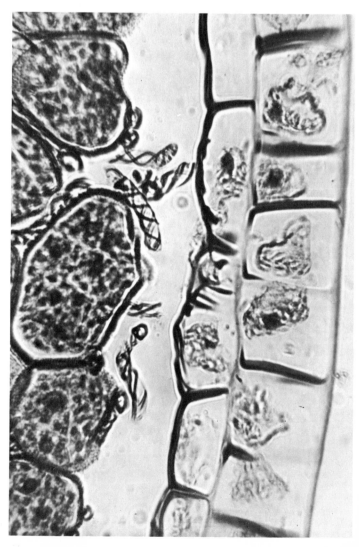

40

Fig. 20.   Studies of the sporogonium of *Pellia epiphylla*

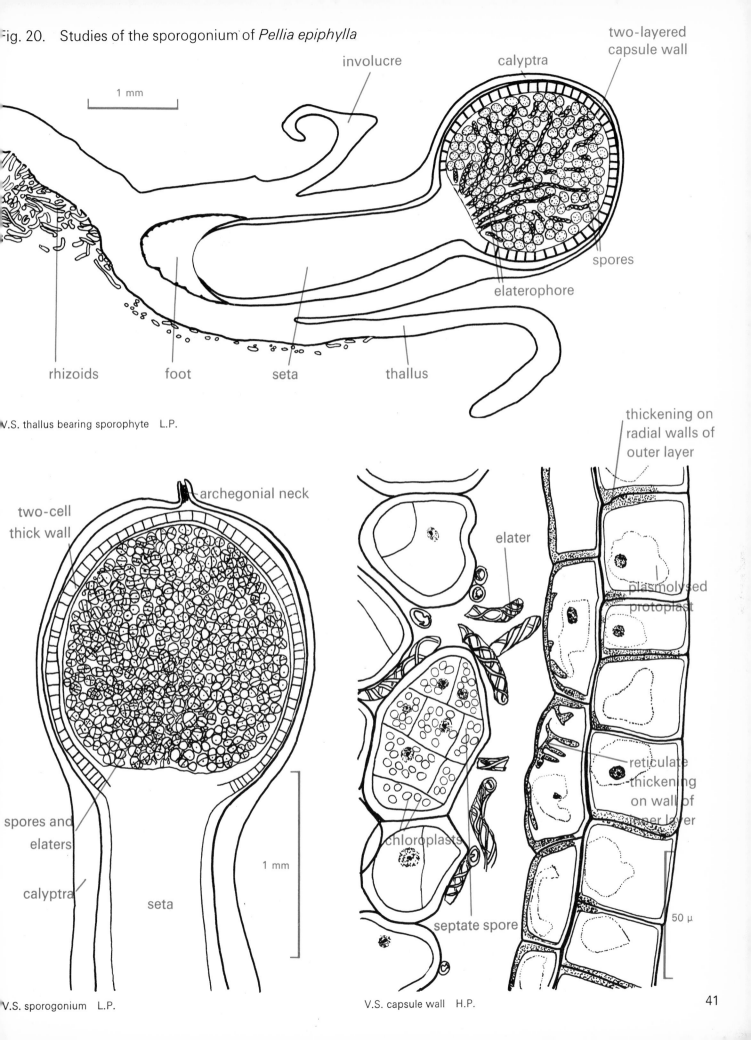

1 mm

involucre

calyptra

two-layered
capsule wall

spores

elaterophore

rhizoids   foot   seta   thallus

V.S. thallus bearing sporophyte   L.P.

two-cell
thick wall

archegonial neck

thickening on
radial walls of
outer layer

elater

plasmolysed
protoplast

reticulate
thickening
on wall of
inner layer

spores and
elaters

calyptra

seta

1 mm

chloroplasts

septate spore

50 μ

V.S. sporogonium   L.P.

V.S. capsule wall   H.P.

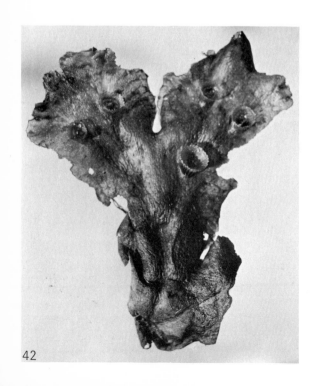
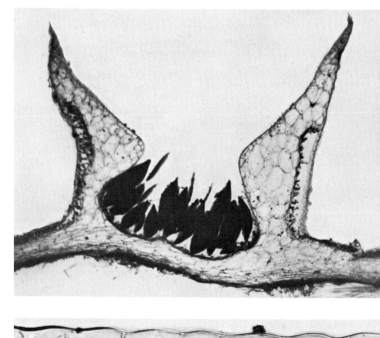
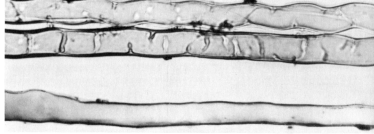

Fig. 21.   Life studies of *Marchantia polymorpha*, MARCHANTIALES

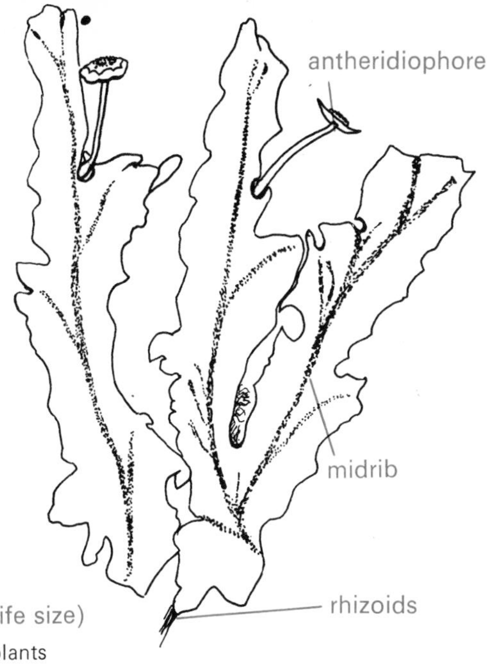

antheridiophore

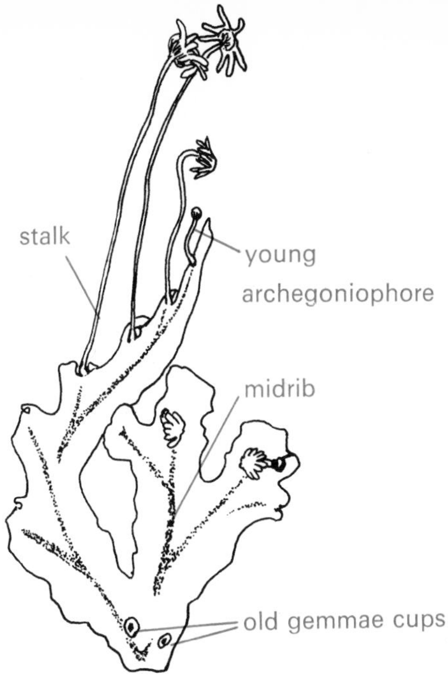

(life size)

stalk

young
archegoniophore

midrib

midrib

old gemmae cups

rhizoids

(life size)

Male plants

Female plant

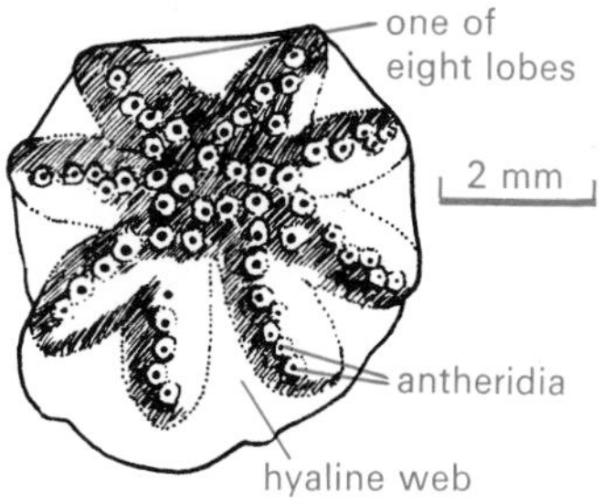

one of
eight lobes

2 mm

one of
nine lobes

2 mm

developing
sporogonium

seta

2 mm

antheridia

groove
containing
rhizoids

dehisced
sporogonium

stalk

hyaline web

Antheridiophore—upper side

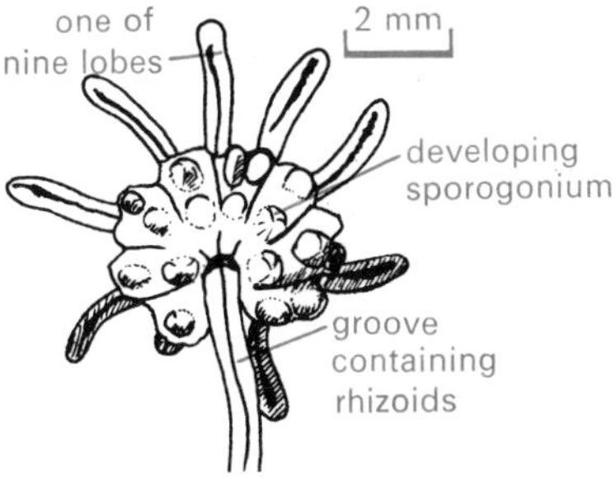

Archegoniophore—lower side

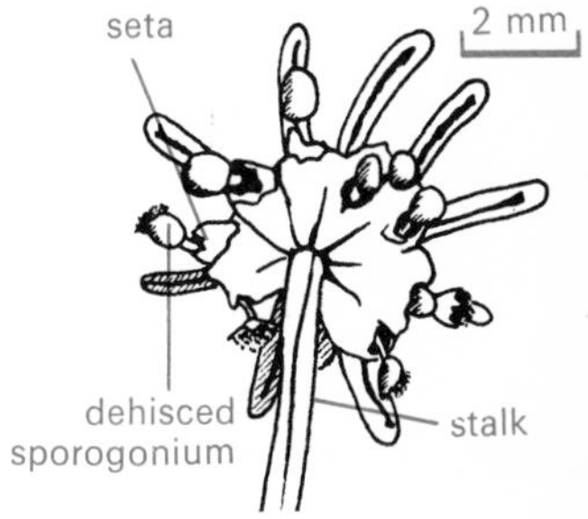

Archegoniophore with mature sporogonia

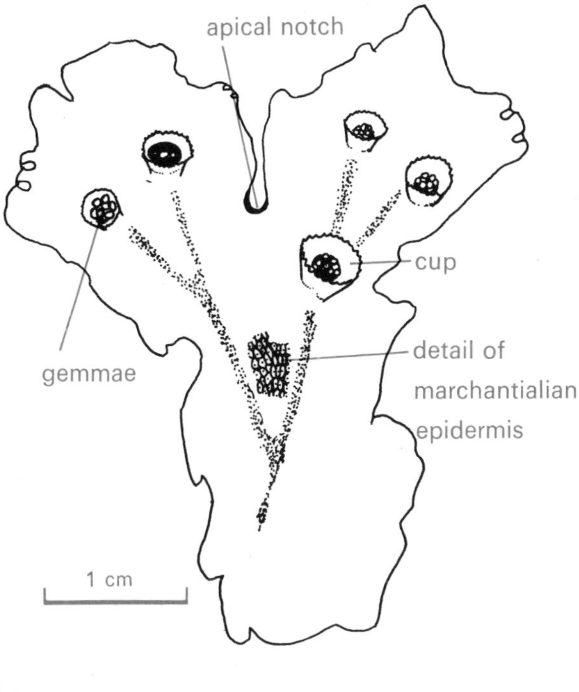

0·5 mm

apical notch

stalk

inner ledge

gemma

cup

pore

detail of
marchantialian
epidermis

gemmae

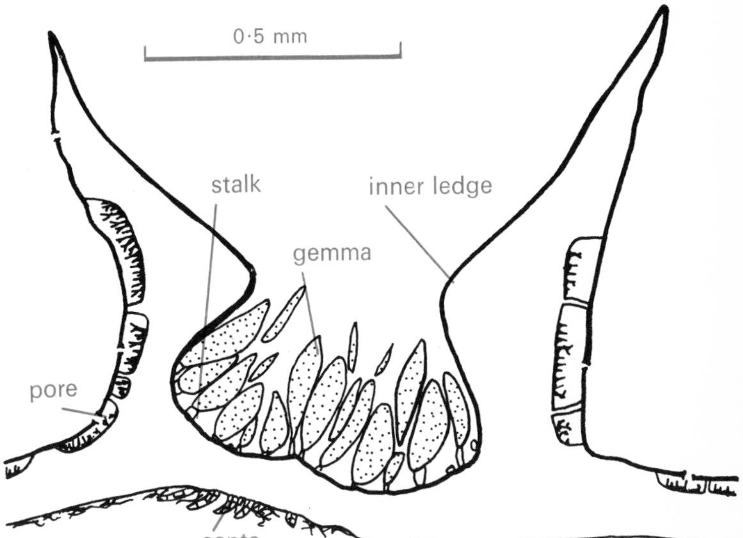

V.S. gemma cup

septa

tubercles

1 cm

20 μ

smooth wall

Plant with gemmae cups

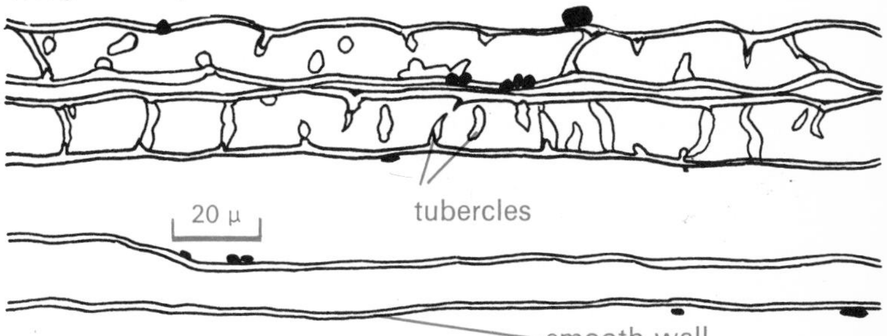

Tuberculate and smooth-walled rhizoids

43

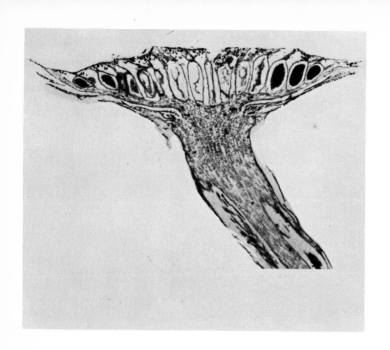
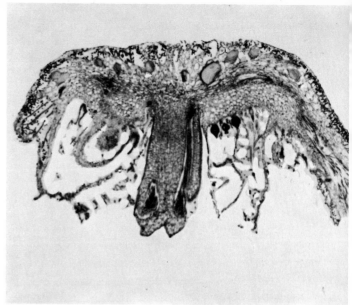
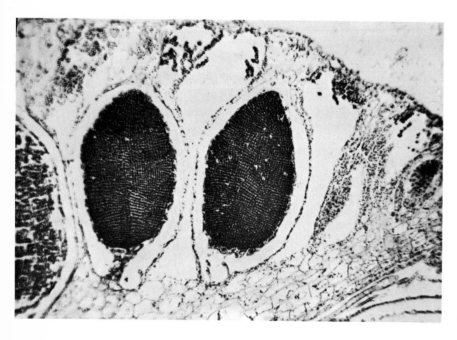
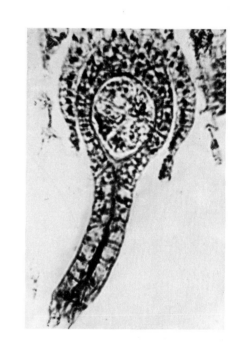
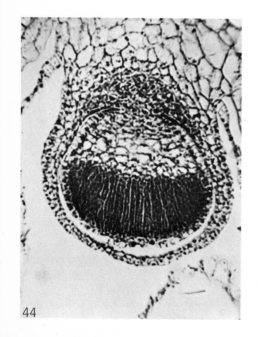
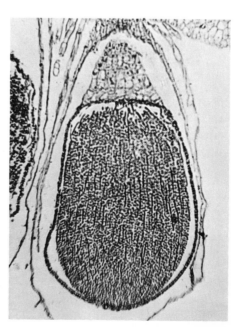
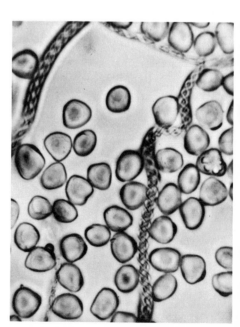

44

Fig. 22. Studies of sexual reproduction in *Marchantia polymorpha*

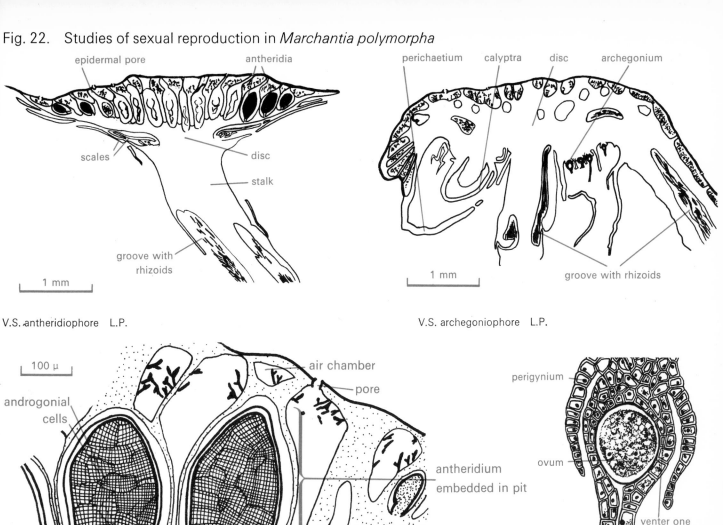

epidermal pore   antheridia

scales   disc

                        stalk

groove with
rhizoids

1 mm

V.S. antheridiophore L.P.

perichaetium   calyptra   disc   archegonium

groove with rhizoids

1 mm

V.S. archegoniophore L.P.

100 μ   air chamber

                        pore

androgonial
cells

jacket   antheridium
                        embedded in pit

tuberculate rhizoid

disc   scale

V.S. antheridiophore H.P.

perigynium

ovum

venter one
to two cells
in thickness

neck cell

remains of
canal cells

50 μ

V.S. archegonium H.P.

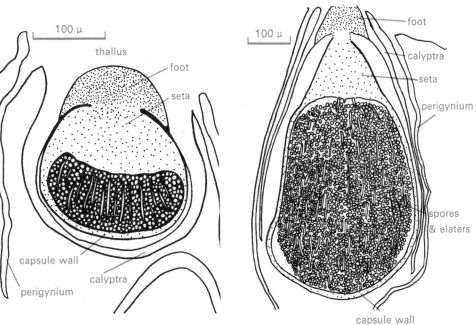

100 μ

thallus   foot

                 seta

capsule wall

calyptra

perigynium

V.S. young sporogonium L.P.

100 μ   foot

                   calyptra

                   seta

                   perigynium

                   spores
                   & elaters

capsule wall

V.S. sporogonium at a later stage L.P.

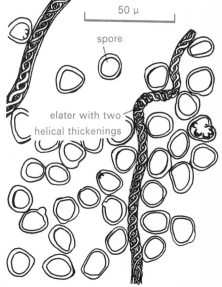

50 μ

spore

elater with two
helical thickenings

Spores and elaters H.P.   45

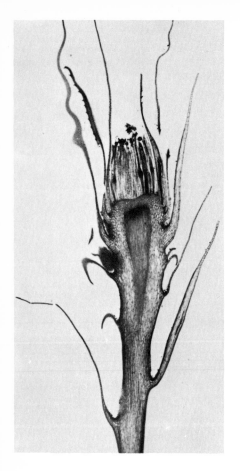

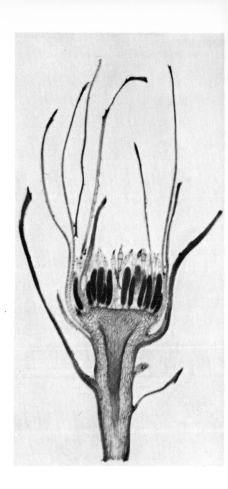

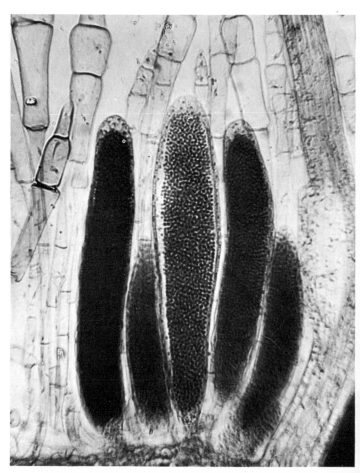

46

Fig. 23.   Studies of the sexual reproductive organs of *Funaria hygrometrica*, BRYALES

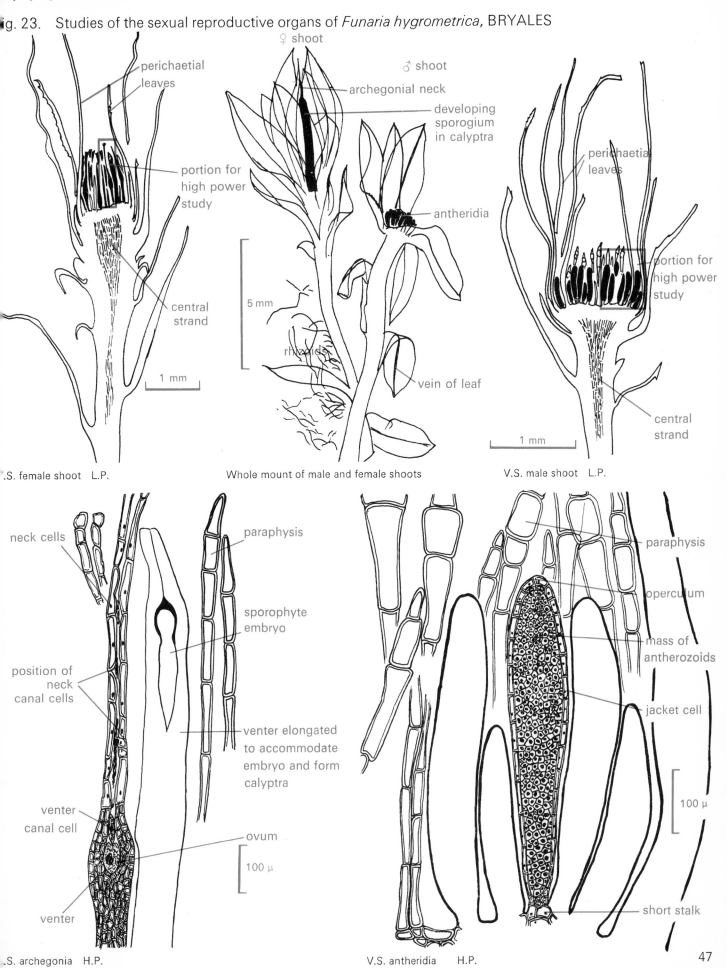

perichaetial leaves

portion for high power study

central strand

♀ shoot

♂ shoot

archegonial neck

developing sporogium in calyptra

antheridia

5 mm

1 mm

rhizoids

vein of leaf

perichaetial leaves

portion for high power study

central strand

1 mm

V.S. female shoot   L.P.

Whole mount of male and female shoots

V.S. male shoot   L.P.

neck cells

paraphysis

position of neck canal cells

sporophyte embryo

venter elongated to accommodate embryo and form calyptra

venter canal cell

ovum

venter

100 μ

paraphysis

operculum

mass of antherozoids

jacket cell

100 μ

short stalk

V.S. archegonia   H.P.

V.S. antheridia   H.P.

47

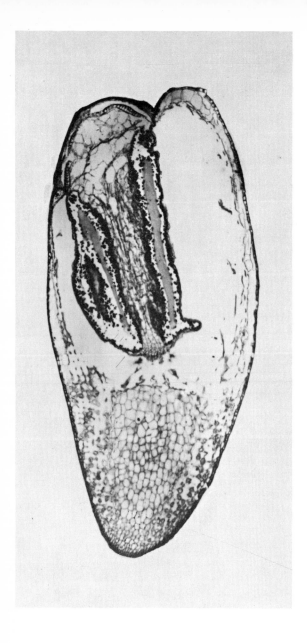

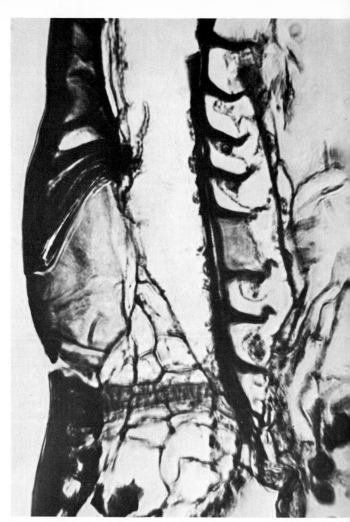

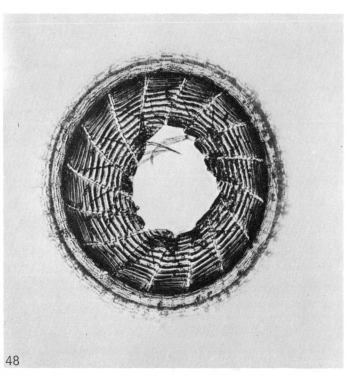

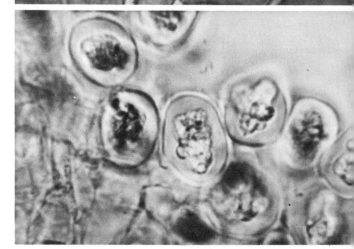

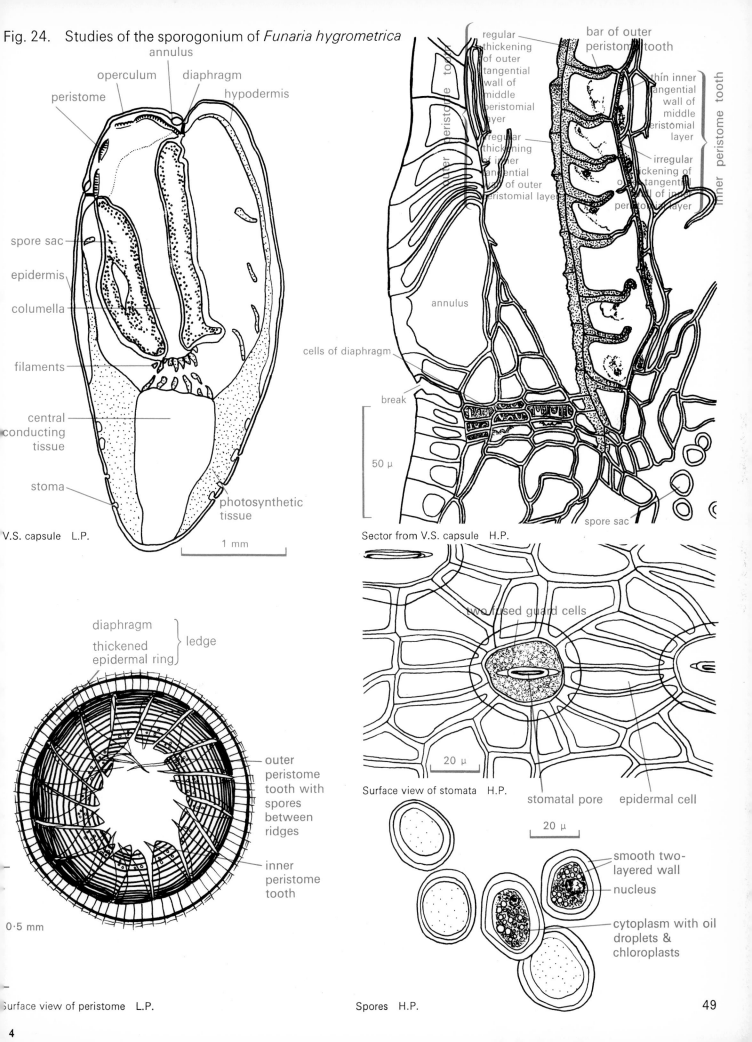

Fig. 24.   Studies of the sporogonium of *Funaria hygrometrica*

annulus
operculum
peristome
diaphragm
hypodermis

spore sac
epidermis
columella
filaments

central
conducting
tissue

stoma
photosynthetic
tissue

V.S. capsule   L.P.

1 mm

regular
thickening
of outer
tangential
wall of
middle
peristomial
layer

bar of outer
peristome tooth

thin inner
tangential
wall of
middle
peristomial
layer

regular
thickening
of inner
tangential
wall of outer
peristomial layer

irregular
thickening of
outer tangential
wall of inner
peristomial layer

outer peristome tooth

inner peristome tooth

annulus

cells of diaphragm

break

50 μ

spore sac

Sector from V.S. capsule   H.P.

diaphragm
thickened
epidermal ring

ledge

outer
peristome
tooth with
spores
between
ridges

inner
peristome
tooth

0·5 mm

Surface view of peristome   L.P.

two fused guard cells

20 μ

Surface view of stomata   H.P.

stomatal pore   epidermal cell

20 μ

smooth two-
layered wall

nucleus

cytoplasm with oil
droplets &
chloroplasts

Spores   H.P.

49

4

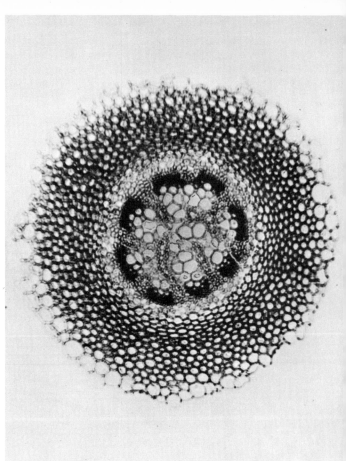

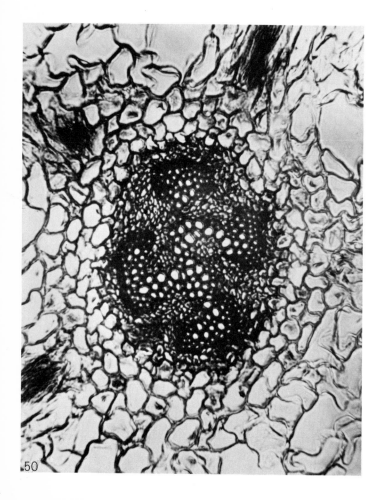

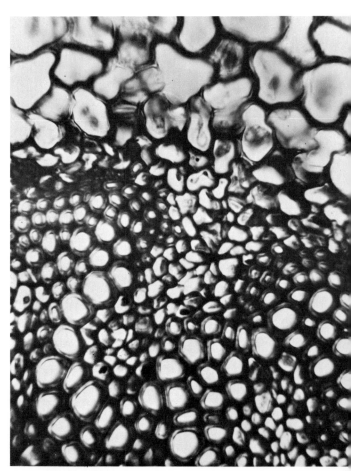

50

Pteridophyta-Lycopodiales

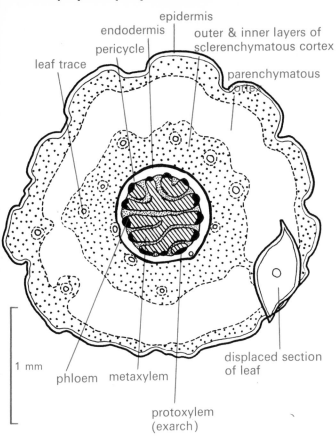

Fig. 25. T.S. stem of *Lycopodium clavatum* (plectostele) L.P.

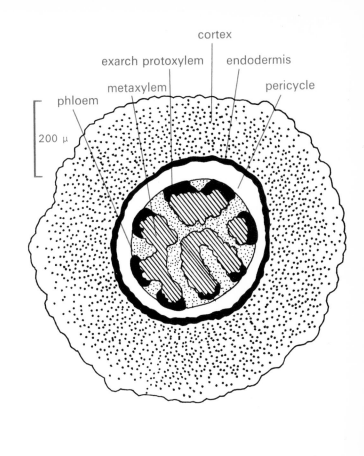

Fig. 26. T.S. old root of *Lycopodium clavatum* (note similarity of stele to that of stem) L.P.

Fig. 27. T.S. stem of *Lycopodium selago* (actinostele) L.P.

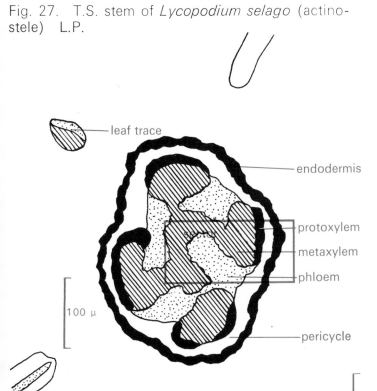

Fig. 28. Sector from fig. 27 H.P.

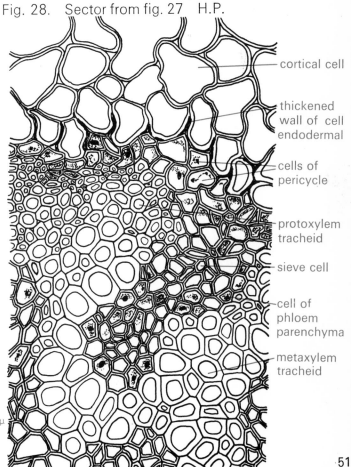

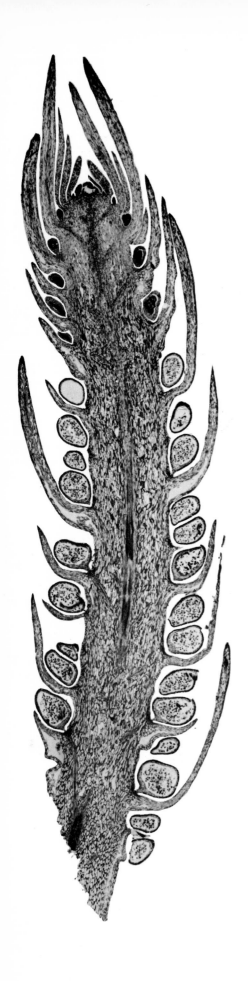

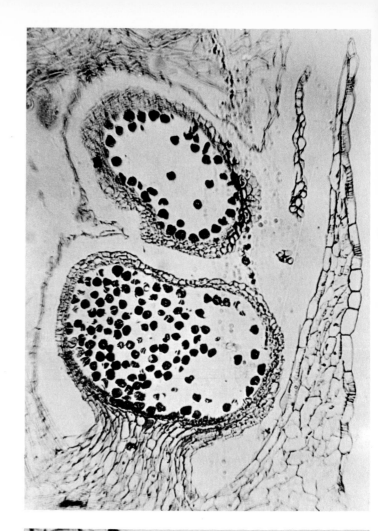

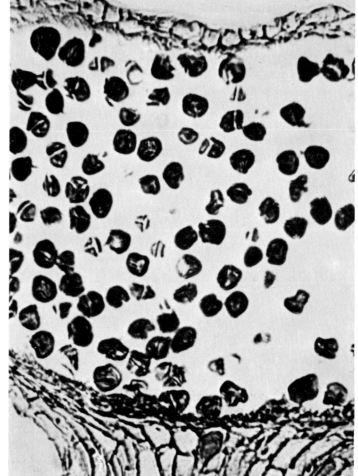

Fig. 29. Studies of the strobilus of *Lycopodium*

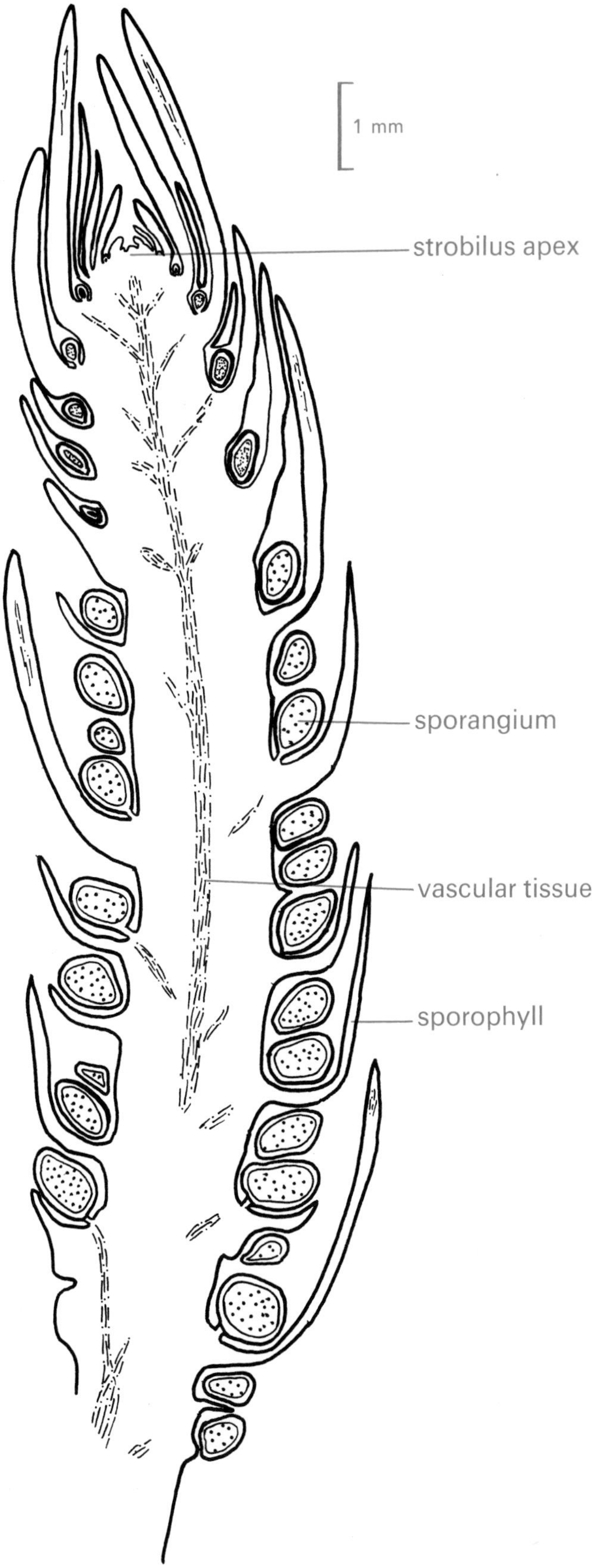

1 mm

strobilus apex

sporangium

vascular tissue

sporophyll

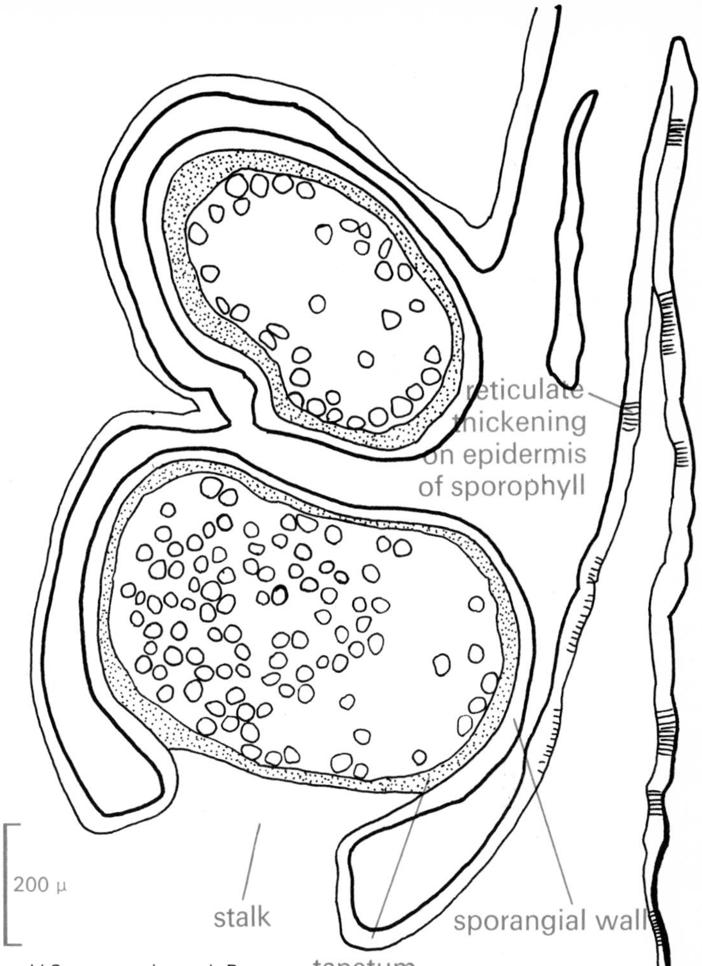

reticulate
thickening
on epidermis
of sporophyll

200 μ

stalk

sporangial wall

tapetum

V.S. sporangium   L.P.

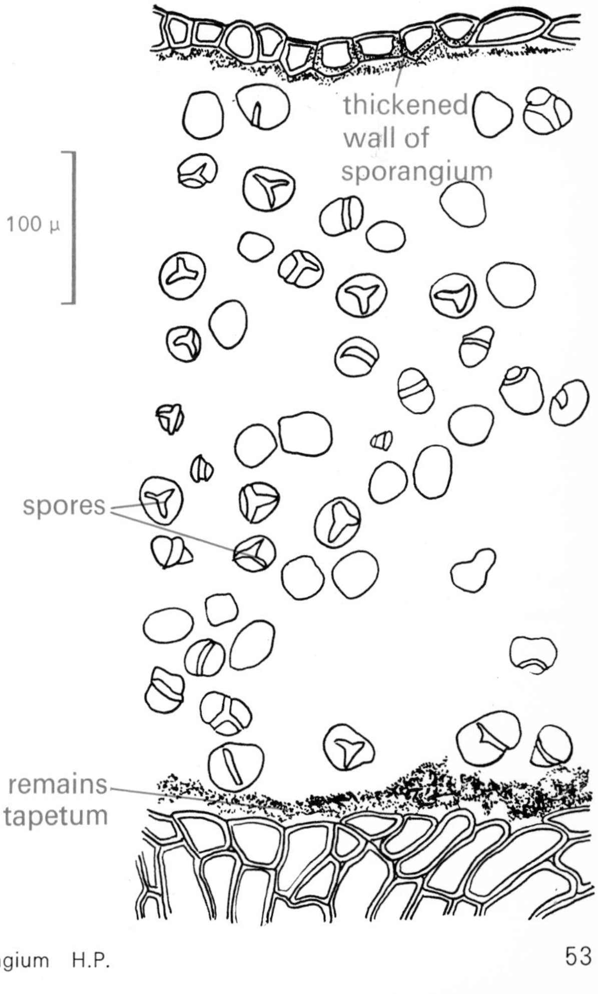

thickened
wall of
sporangium

100 μ

spores

remains
of tapetum

V.S. strobilus   L.P.

V.S. sporangium   H.P.

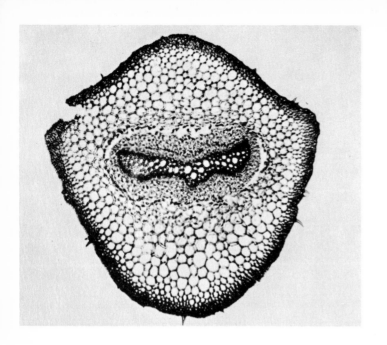

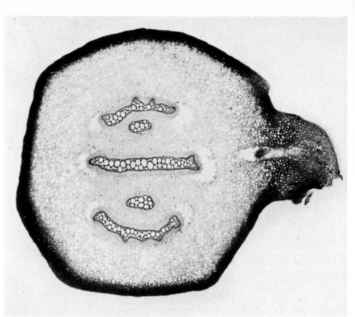

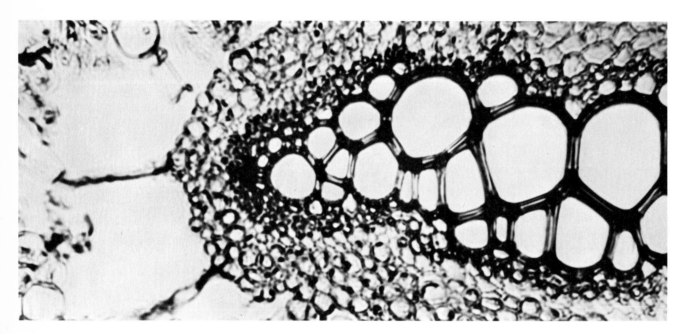

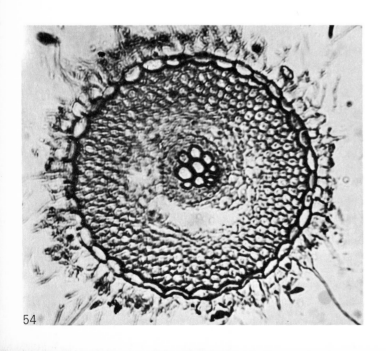

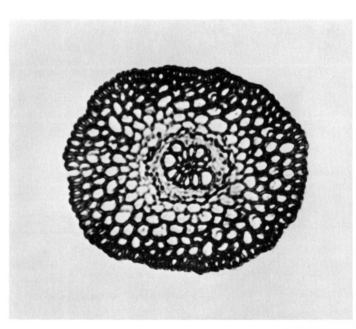

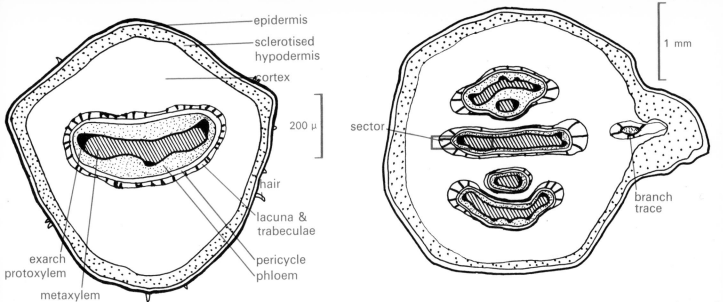

Fig. 30. T.S. stem of a monostelic species of *Selaginella* Sp. L.P.

Fig. 31. T.S. stem of a polystelic species of *Selaginella* Sp. L.P.

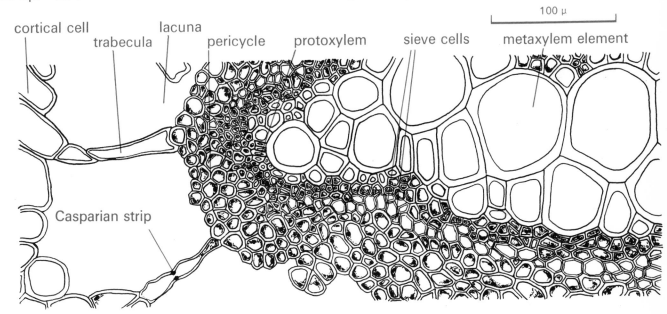

Fig. 32. Sector from fig. 31 L.P.

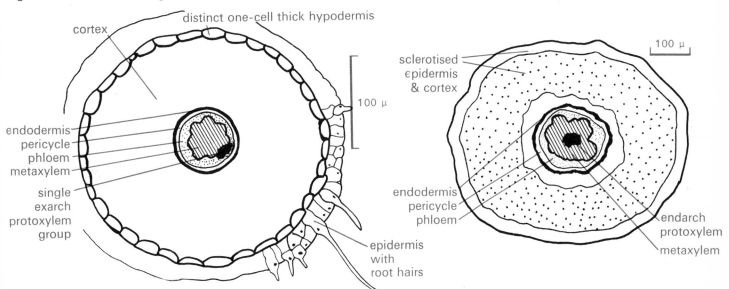

Fig. 33. T.S. root of *Selaginella* Sp. L.P.

Fig. 34. T.S. rhizophore of *Selaginella* Sp. L.P.   55

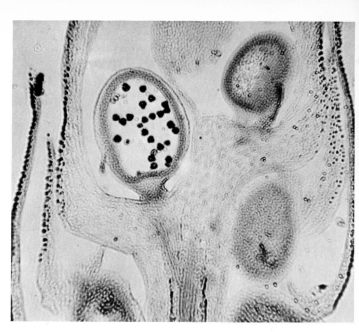

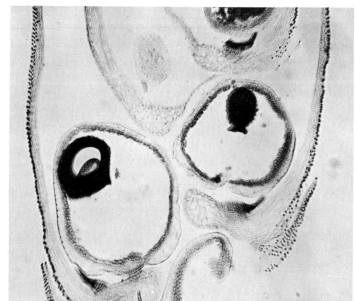

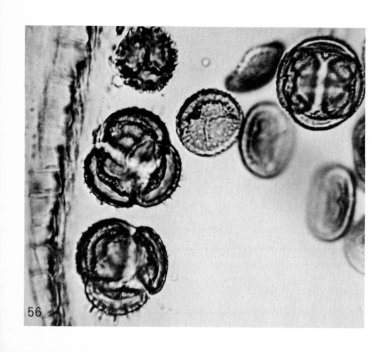

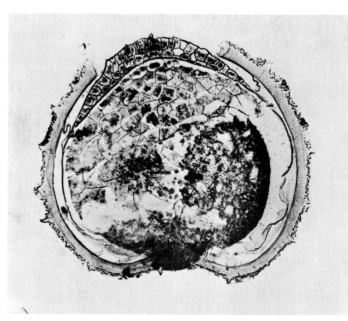

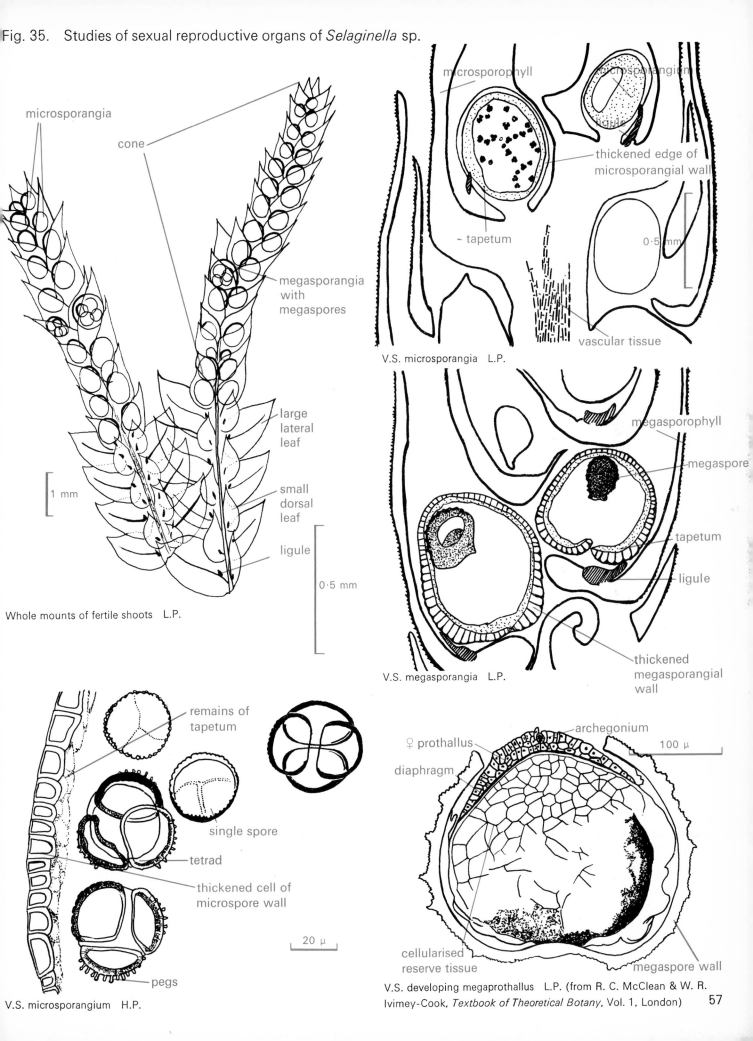

Fig. 35.   Studies of sexual reproductive organs of *Selaginella* sp.

microsporangia

cone

megasporangia with megaspores

large lateral leaf

small dorsal leaf

ligule

1 mm

0·5 mm

Whole mounts of fertile shoots   L.P.

microsporophyll

microsporangium

thickened edge of microsporangial wall

tapetum

ligule

0·5 mm

vascular tissue

V.S. microsporangia   L.P.

megasporophyll

megaspore

tapetum

ligule

thickened megasporangial wall

V.S. megasporangia   L.P.

remains of tapetum

single spore

tetrad

thickened cell of microspore wall

pegs

20 μ

V.S. microsporangium   H.P.

♀ prothallus

diaphragm

archegonium

100 μ

cellularised reserve tissue

megaspore wall

V.S. developing megaprothallus   L.P. (from R. C. McClean & W. R. Ivimey-Cook, *Textbook of Theoretical Botany*, Vol. 1, London)

57

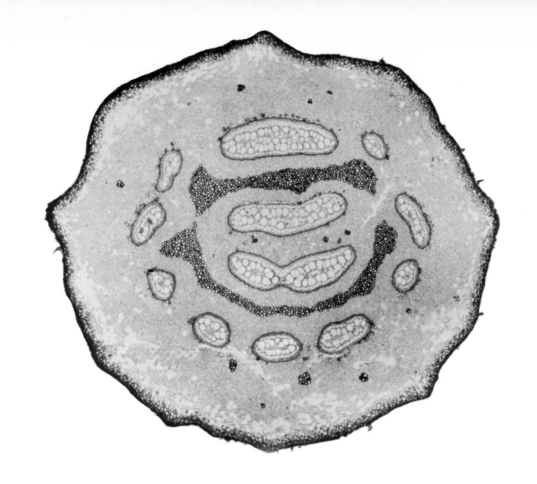

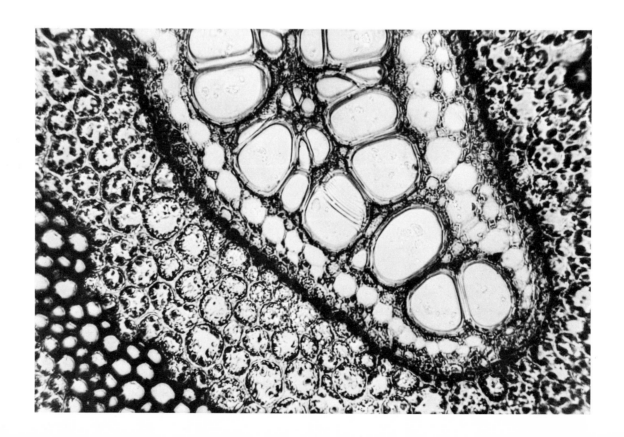

Pteridophyta-Filicales

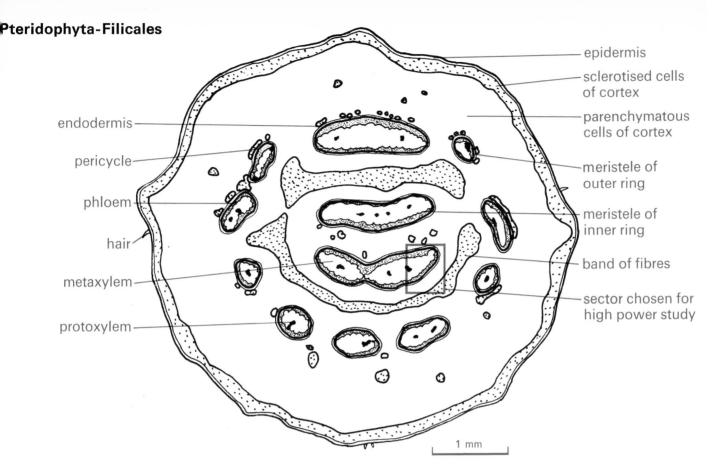

epidermis
sclerotised cells of cortex
parenchymatous cells of cortex
meristele of outer ring
meristele of inner ring
band of fibres
sector chosen for high power study

endodermis
pericycle
phloem
hair
metaxylem
protoxylem

1 mm

Fig. 36.   *Pteridium aquilinum*—T.S. of a rhizome   L.P.

Fig. 37.   *Pteridium aquilinum*—portion of a meristele in T.S.   H.P.

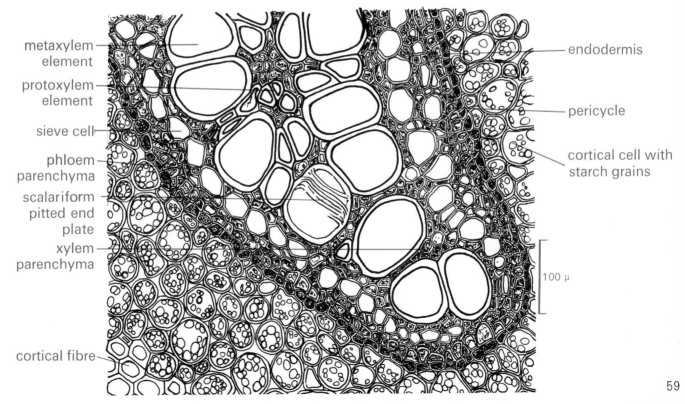

metaxylem element
protoxylem element
sieve cell
phloem parenchyma
scalariform pitted end plate
xylem parenchyma
cortical fibre

endodermis
pericycle
cortical cell with starch grains

100 μ

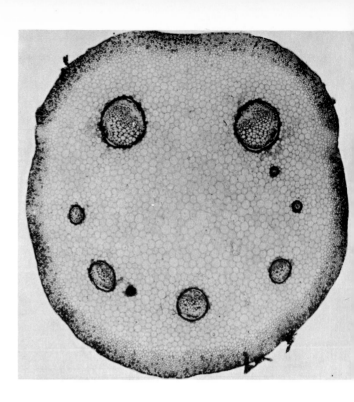

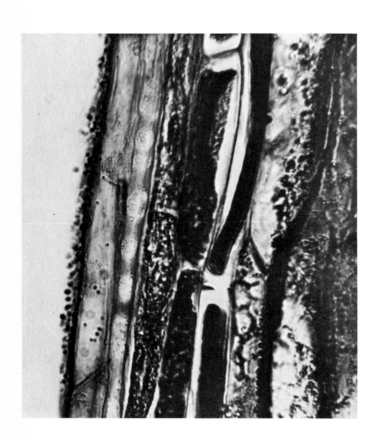

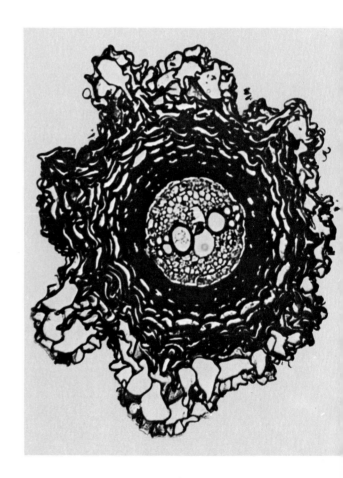

Fig. 38. Studies of vegetative structure in Filicales

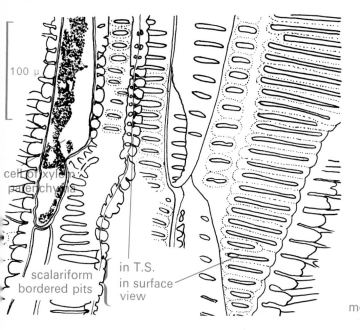

100 μ

cell of xylem
parenchyma

scalariform
bordered pits

in T.S.

in surface
view

Pteridium—L.S. tracheids from rhizome   H.P.

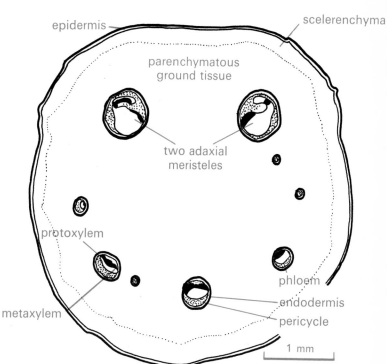

epidermis

scelerenchyma

parenchymatous
ground tissue

two adaxial
meristeles

protoxylem

phloem

endodermis

pericycle

metaxylem

1 mm

Dryopteris--T.S. petiole   L.P.

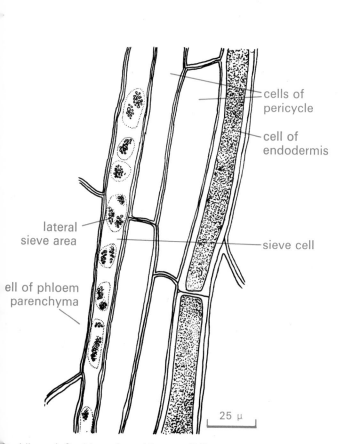

cells of
pericycle

cell of
endodermis

sieve cell

lateral
sieve area

cell of phloem
parenchyma

25 μ

Pteridium—L.S. phloem from rhizome   H.P.

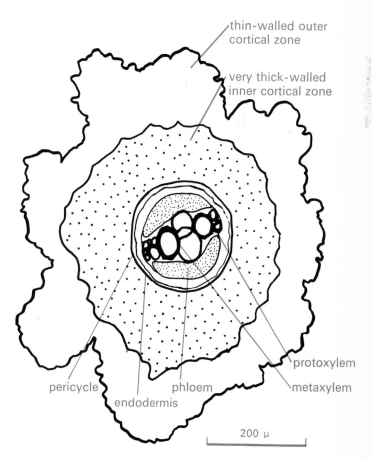

thin-walled outer
cortical zone

very thick-walled
inner cortical zone

protoxylem

metaxylem

pericycle

phloem

endodermis

200 μ

Dryopteris—T.S. root   L.P.

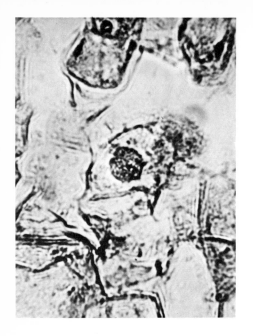 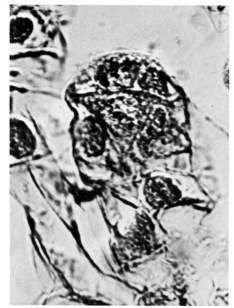 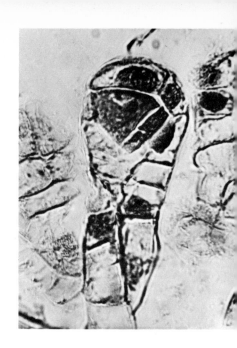

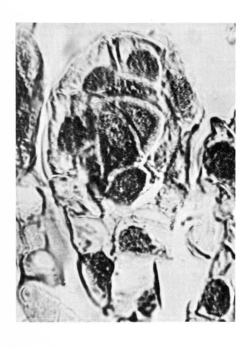 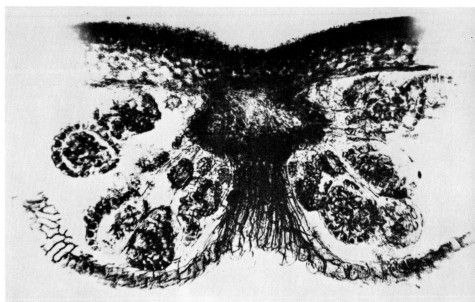

62

Fig. 39. Studies of the sporangium of *Dryopteris filix-mas*

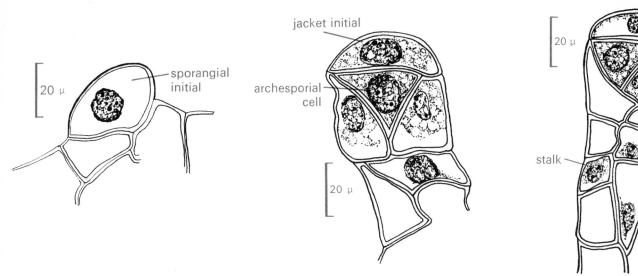

20 μ — sporangial initial

Sporangial initiation

jacket initial
archesporial cell
20 μ

Formation of four-sided archesporial cell

jacket initials
20 μ
tapetal initial
stalk

First division of archesporial cell

jacket cell
one of four tapetal initials
products of first division of primary sporogenous cell
20 μ

First division of primary sporogenous cell

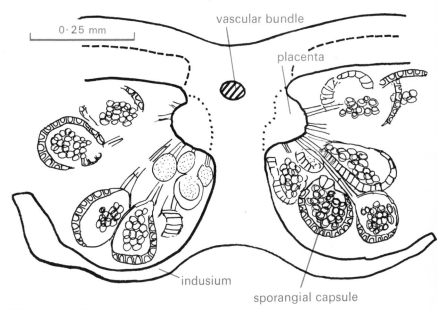

0·25 mm
vascular bundle
placenta
indusium
sporangial capsule

V.S. sorus   L.P.

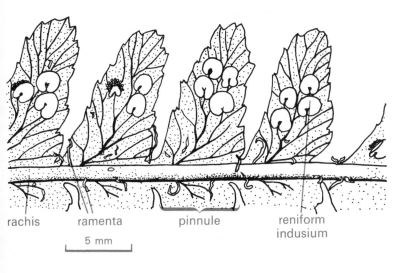

rachis   ramenta   pinnule   reniform indusium

5 mm

Lower side of fertile pinna—living

0·5 mm
annulus   stomium
cut surface of indusium

Sorus with indusium removed—living

63

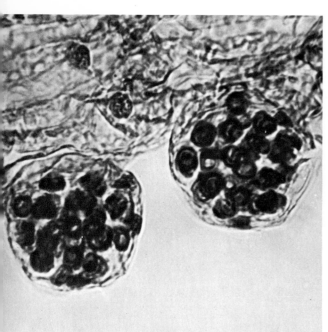
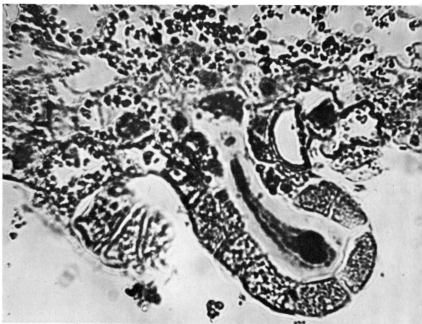

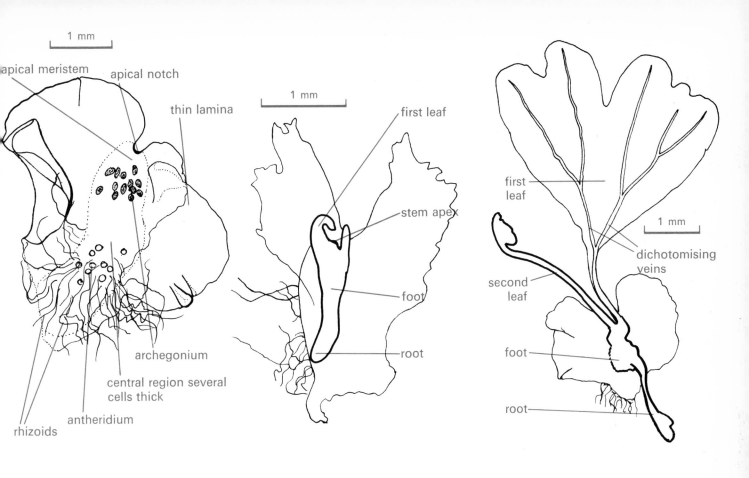

Fig. 40. *Dryopteris filix-mas*—prothallus and development of sporophyte   L.P.

Fig. 41. Studies of the sexual reproductive organs of *Dryopteris filix-mas*

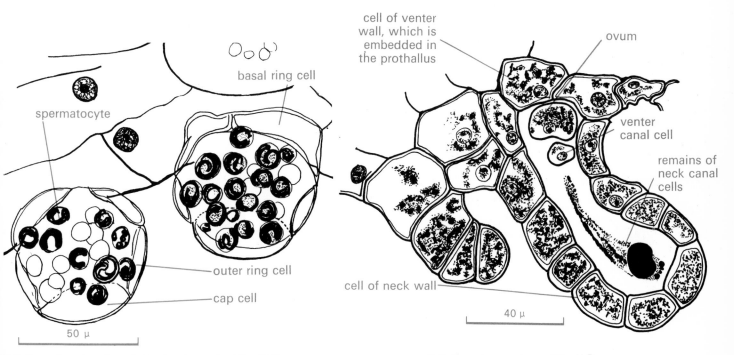

V.S. through region of prothallus bearing antheridia   H.P.

V.S. through an archegonium   H.P.

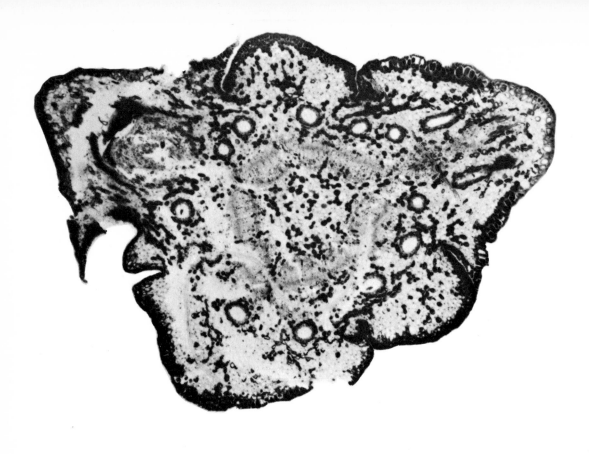

Gymnospermae

leaf trace

leaf trace

axillary bud

phloem

cambium

secondary xylem

primary ray

pith

primary xylem

resin canals

cortex

epidermis

1 mm

Fig. 42. *Pinus sylvestris*—low power study of a transverse section through a one-year-old shoot

Fig. 43. *Pinus sylvestris*—low power study of a transverse section through an old stem

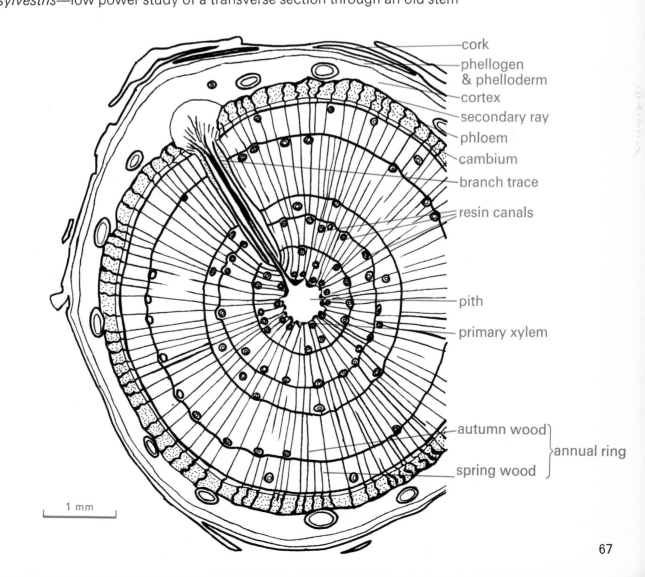

cork

phellogen & phelloderm

cortex

secondary ray

phloem

cambium

branch trace

resin canals

pith

primary xylem

autumn wood

annual ring

spring wood

1 mm

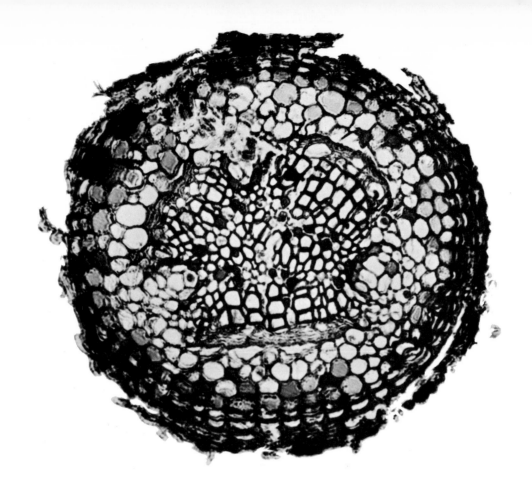

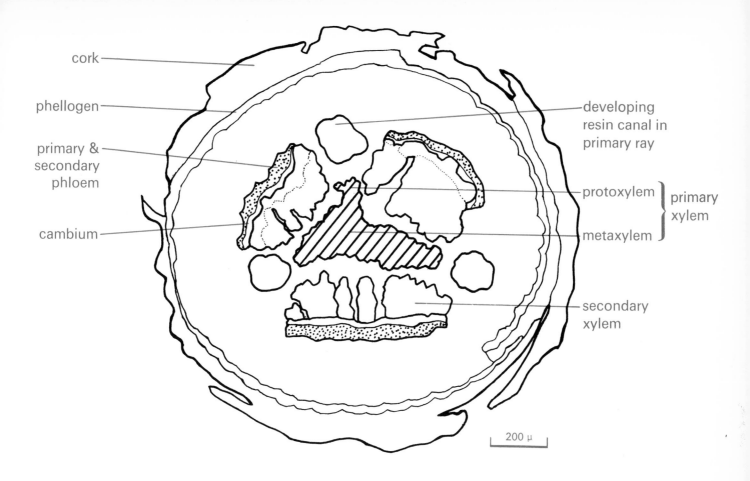

cork

phellogen

primary &
secondary
phloem

cambium

developing
resin canal in
primary ray

protoxylem ⎫
⎬ primary
⎫ xylem
metaxylem ⎭

secondary
xylem

200 μ

Fig. 44. *Pinus sylvestris*—T.S. of a young root   L.P.
Fig. 45. *Pinus sylvestris*—T.S. of an older root   L.P.

rhytidome

cortex

phloem

cambium

secondary ray

primary ray

resin
canals

primary xylem

secondary xylem

differentiating
secondary xylem

500 μ

69

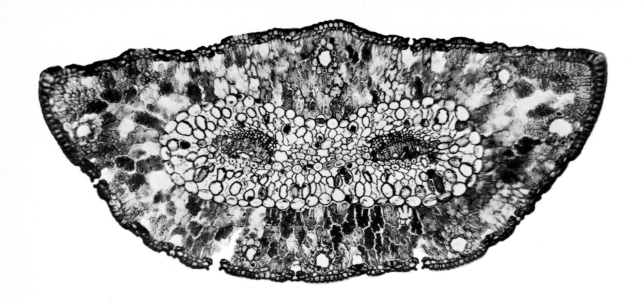

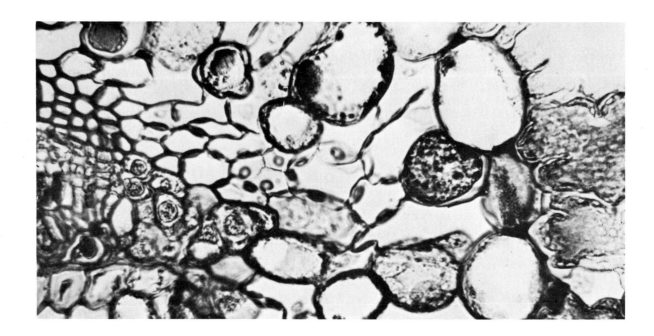

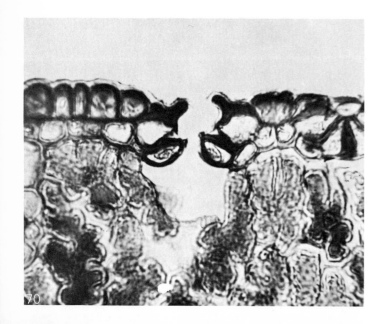

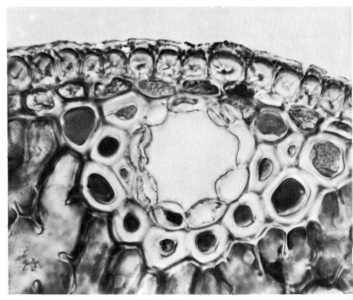

Fig. 46. Studies of the leaf of *Pinus sylvestris*

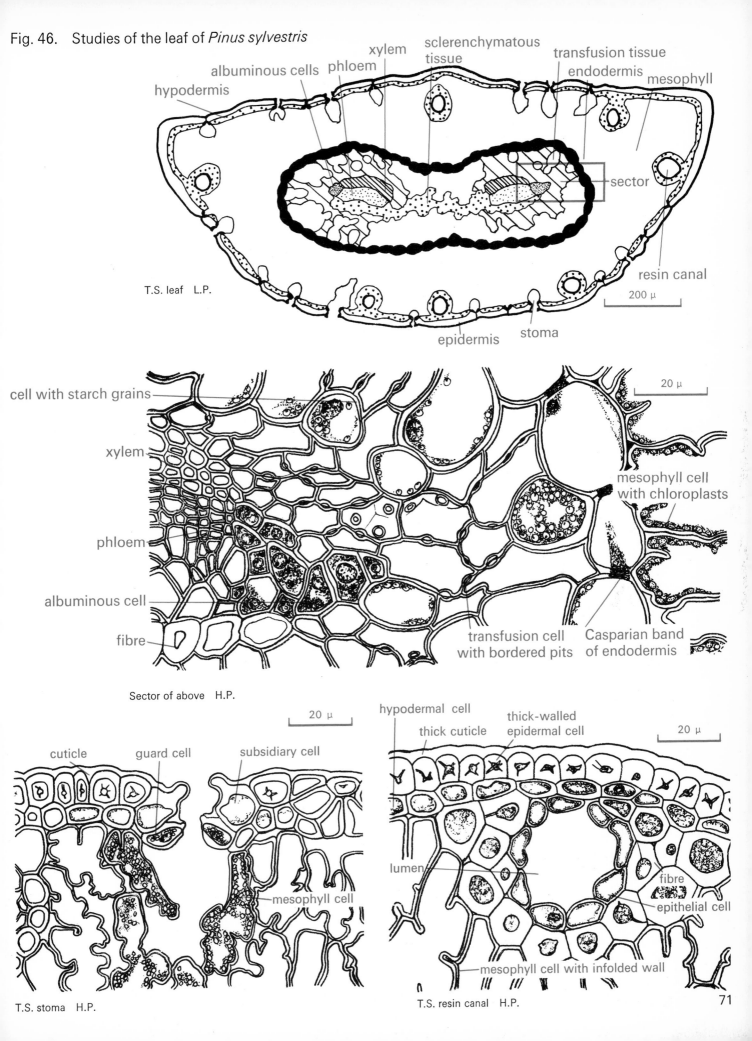

hypodermis

albuminous cells

phloem

xylem

sclerenchymatous tissue

transfusion tissue

endodermis

mesophyll

sector

resin canal

T.S. leaf L.P.

200 μ

epidermis

stoma

cell with starch grains

20 μ

xylem

mesophyll cell with chloroplasts

phloem

albuminous cell

fibre

transfusion cell with bordered pits

Casparian band of endodermis

Sector of above   H.P.

20 μ

cuticle

guard cell

subsidiary cell

mesophyll cell

T.S. stoma H.P.

hypodermal cell

thick cuticle

thick-walled epidermal cell

20 μ

lumen

fibre

epithelial cell

mesophyll cell with infolded wall

T.S. resin canal H.P.

71

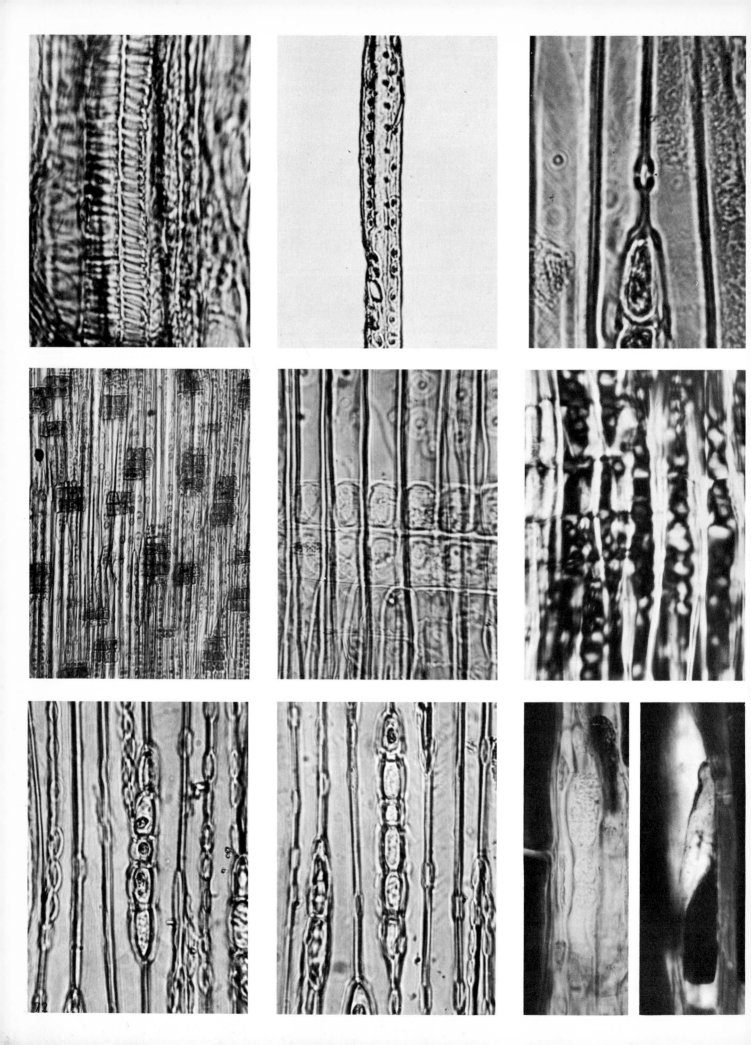

Fig. 47. Studies of the internal anatomy of the stem of *Pinus sylvestris*

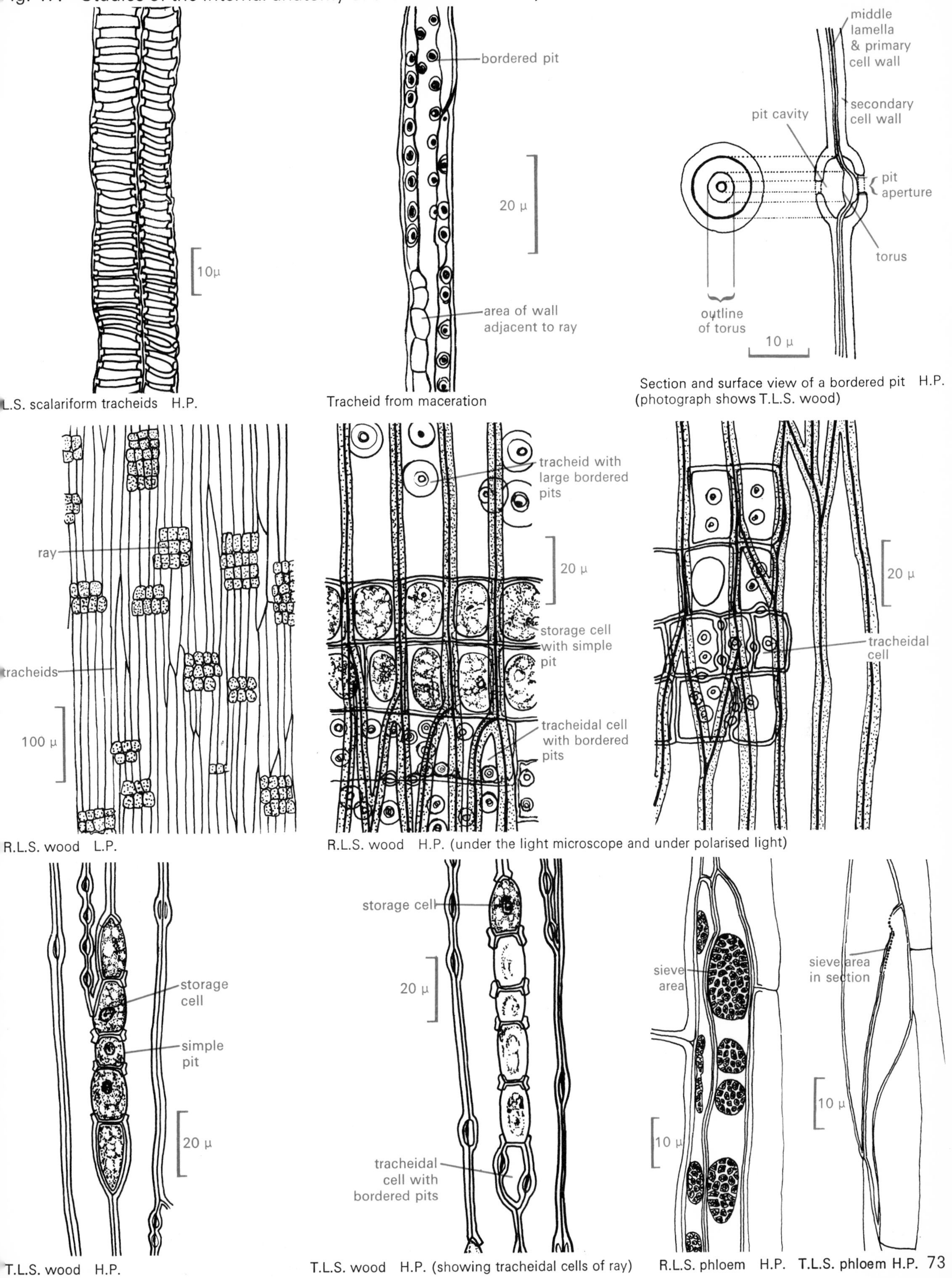

bordered pit

20 μ

area of wall
adjacent to ray

10μ

L.S. scalariform tracheids   H.P.

Tracheid from maceration

middle
lamella
& primary
cell wall

secondary
cell wall

pit cavity

pit
aperture

outline
of torus

torus

10 μ

Section and surface view of a bordered pit   H.P.
(photograph shows T.L.S. wood)

ray

tracheids

100 μ

R.L.S. wood   L.P.

tracheid with
large bordered
pits

20 μ

storage cell
with simple
pit

tracheidal cell
with bordered
pits

R.L.S. wood   H.P. (under the light microscope and under polarised light)

20 μ

tracheidal
cell

storage
cell

simple
pit

20 μ

T.L.S. wood   H.P.

storage cell

20 μ

tracheidal
cell with
bordered pits

T.L.S. wood   H.P. (showing tracheidal cells of ray)

sieve
area

10 μ

R.L.S. phloem   H.P.

sieve area
in section

10 μ

T.L.S. phloem H.P.   73

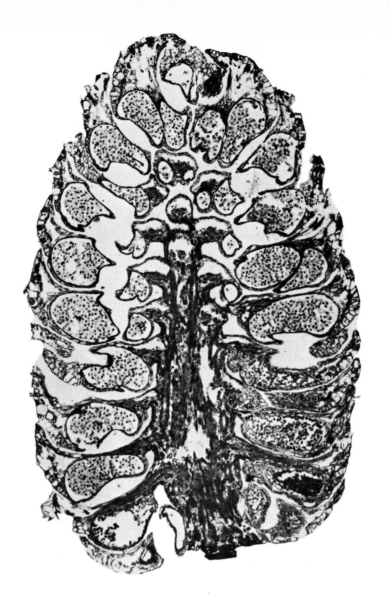

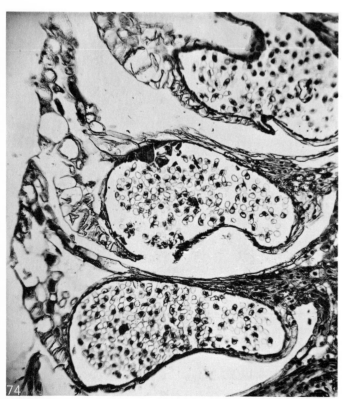

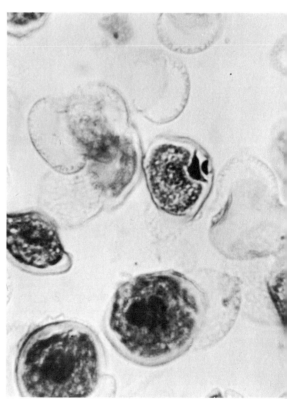

74

Fig. 48. *Pinus sylvestris*—studies of a mature male cone

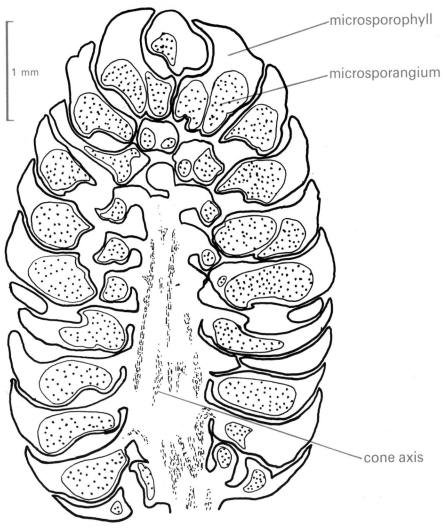

microsporophyll

microsporangium

1 mm

cone axis

V.S. mature male cone   L.P.

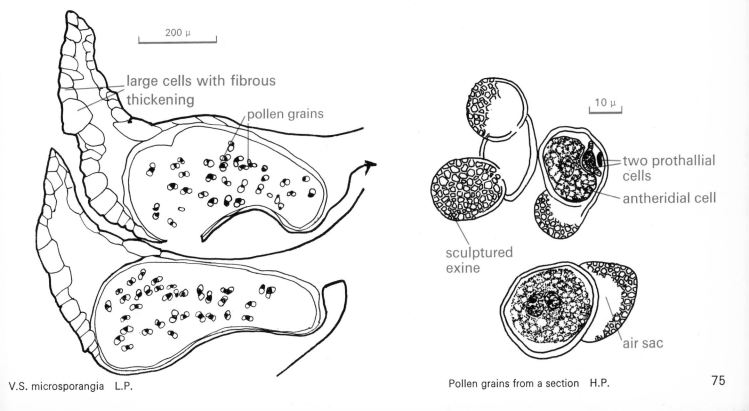

200 μ

large cells with fibrous thickening

pollen grains

10 μ

two prothallial cells

antheridial cell

sculptured exine

air sac

V.S. microsporangia   L.P.

Pollen grains from a section   H.P.

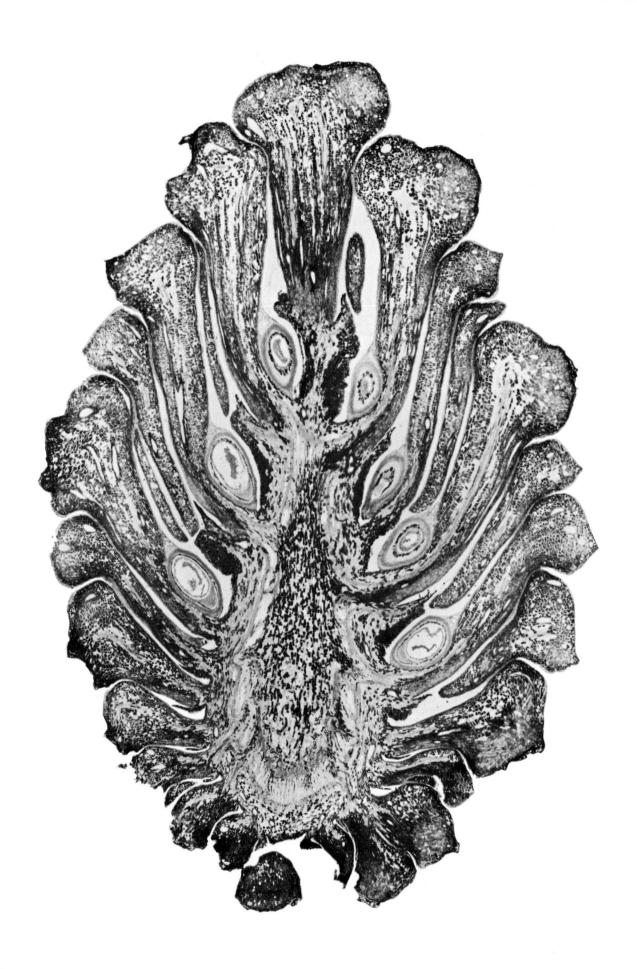

Fig. 49. Vertical section through a two-year old female cone of *Pinus sylvestris*   L.P.

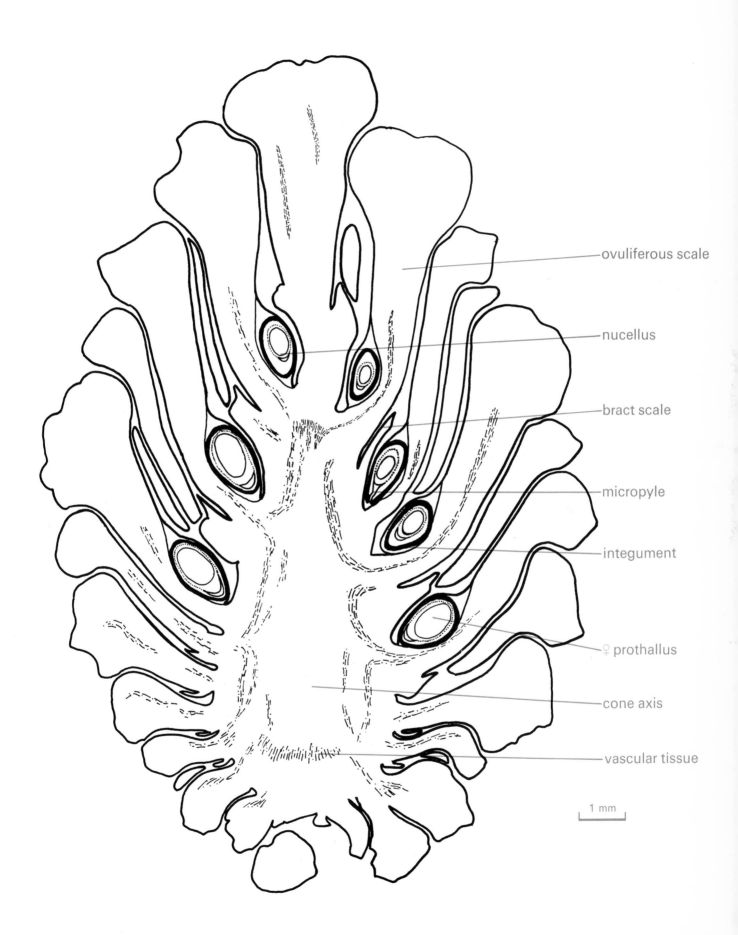

ovuliferous scale

nucellus

bract scale

micropyle

integument

♀ prothallus

cone axis

vascular tissue

1 mm

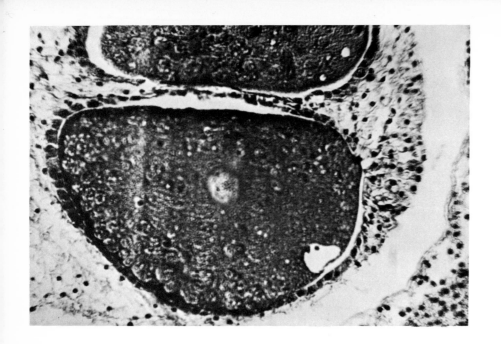

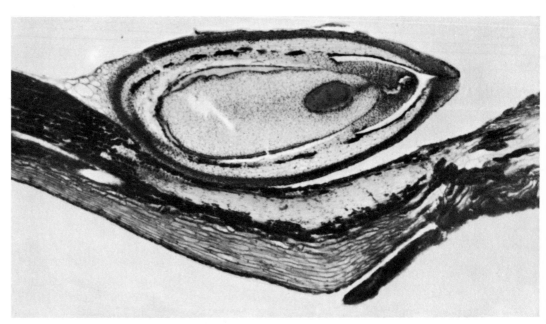

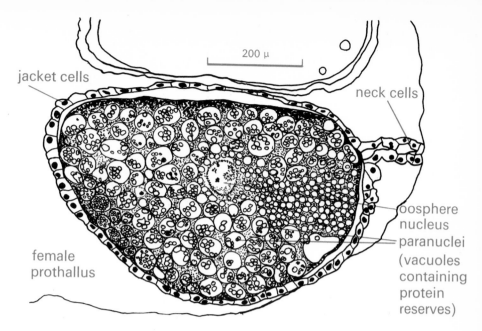

jacket cells

200 µ

neck cells

oosphere
nucleus

paranuclei
(vacuoles
containing
protein
reserves)

female
prothallus

Fig. 50.   *Pinus sylvestris*—V.S. of an archegonium   H.P.

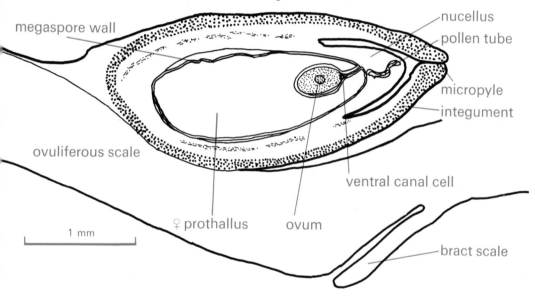

megaspore wall

nucellus

pollen tube

micropyle

integument

ovuliferous scale

ventral canal cell

1 mm

♀ prothallus

ovum

bract scale

Fig. 51.   *Pinus sylvestris*—V.S. of an ovule after fertilisation   L.P.

Fig. 52.   *Pinus sylvestris*—V.S. of a seed   L.P.

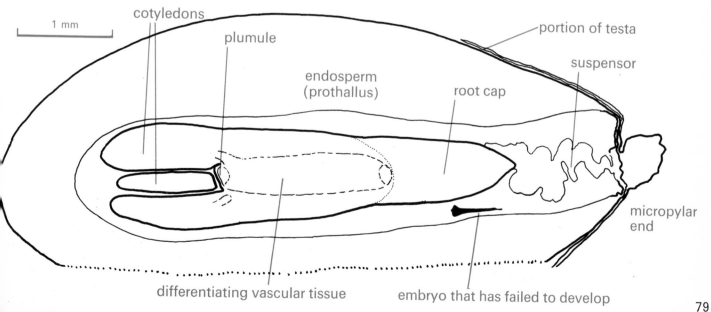

1 mm

cotyledons

plumule

portion of testa

suspensor

endosperm
(prothallus)

root cap

micropylar
end

differentiating vascular tissue

embryo that has failed to develop

Index